# Adult Coloring Book

## Henna Paisley Designs #2

ISBN-13: 978-1532707766

ISBN-10: 1532707762

All enquiries, contact

Hobby Habitat Coloring

contact@hobbyhabitat.com

# Get a FREE Coloring Book

Coloring book fan?

Get a free coloring book from the website bellow:

## www.hobbyhabitat.com/freecoloringbook

Hello and thank you for buying Henna Designs Coloring Book #2.

This is our second book dedicated to beautiful Henna Paisley designs, so if you are a fan or just a first time colorist we are sure you will find these designs as beautiful as we do.

Most coloring pages in this coloring book are flowers and garden related so you can be sure these adult coloring motives will help you relax and unwind after a hard day's work.

We hope that you enjoy coloring these wonderful stress relieving patterns as much as we enjoyed putting them together for you.

Once again thank you for buying our book, and enjoy coloring with Hobby Habitat's adult coloring books.

Thank you!

Hobby Habitat Coloring Books

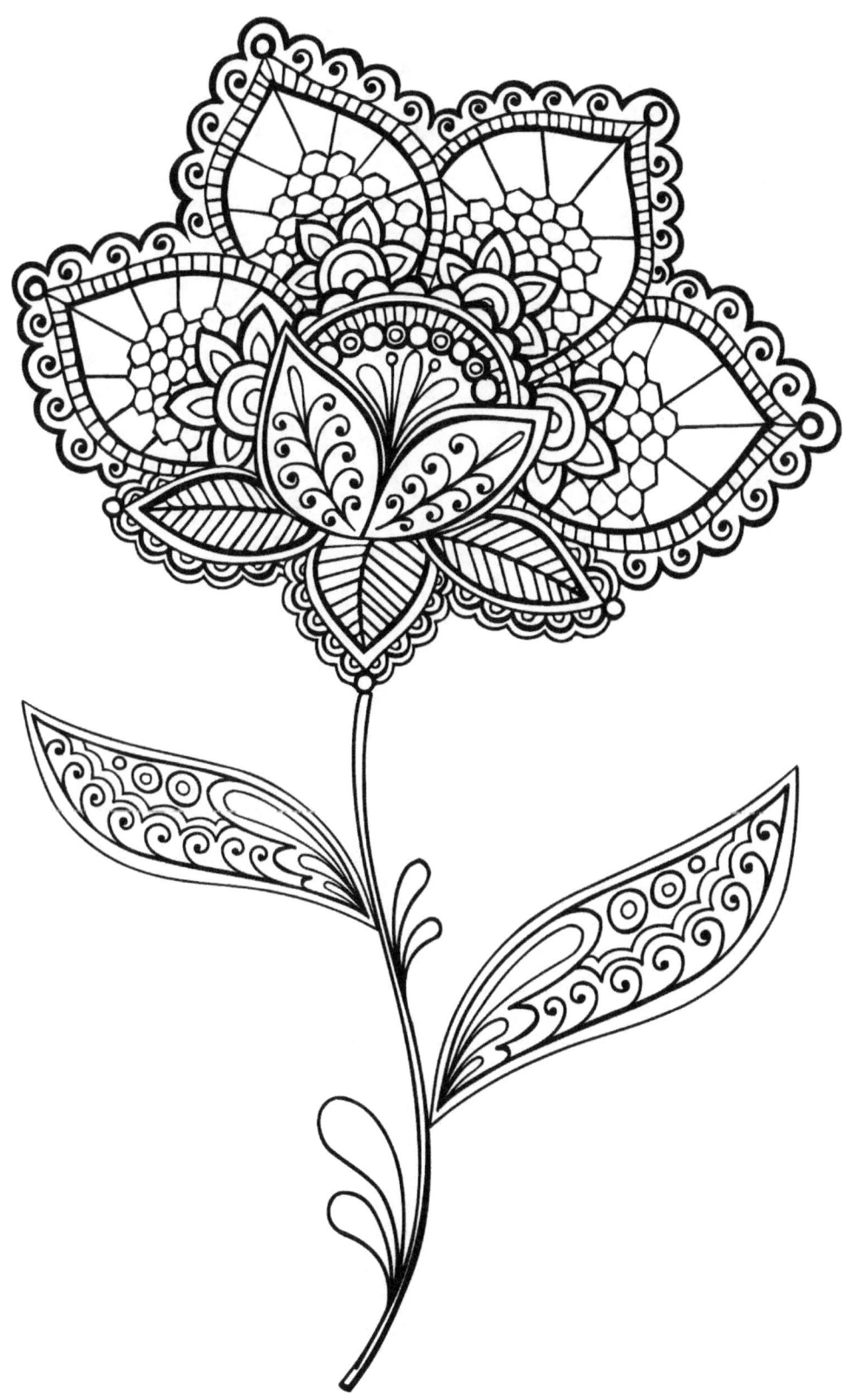

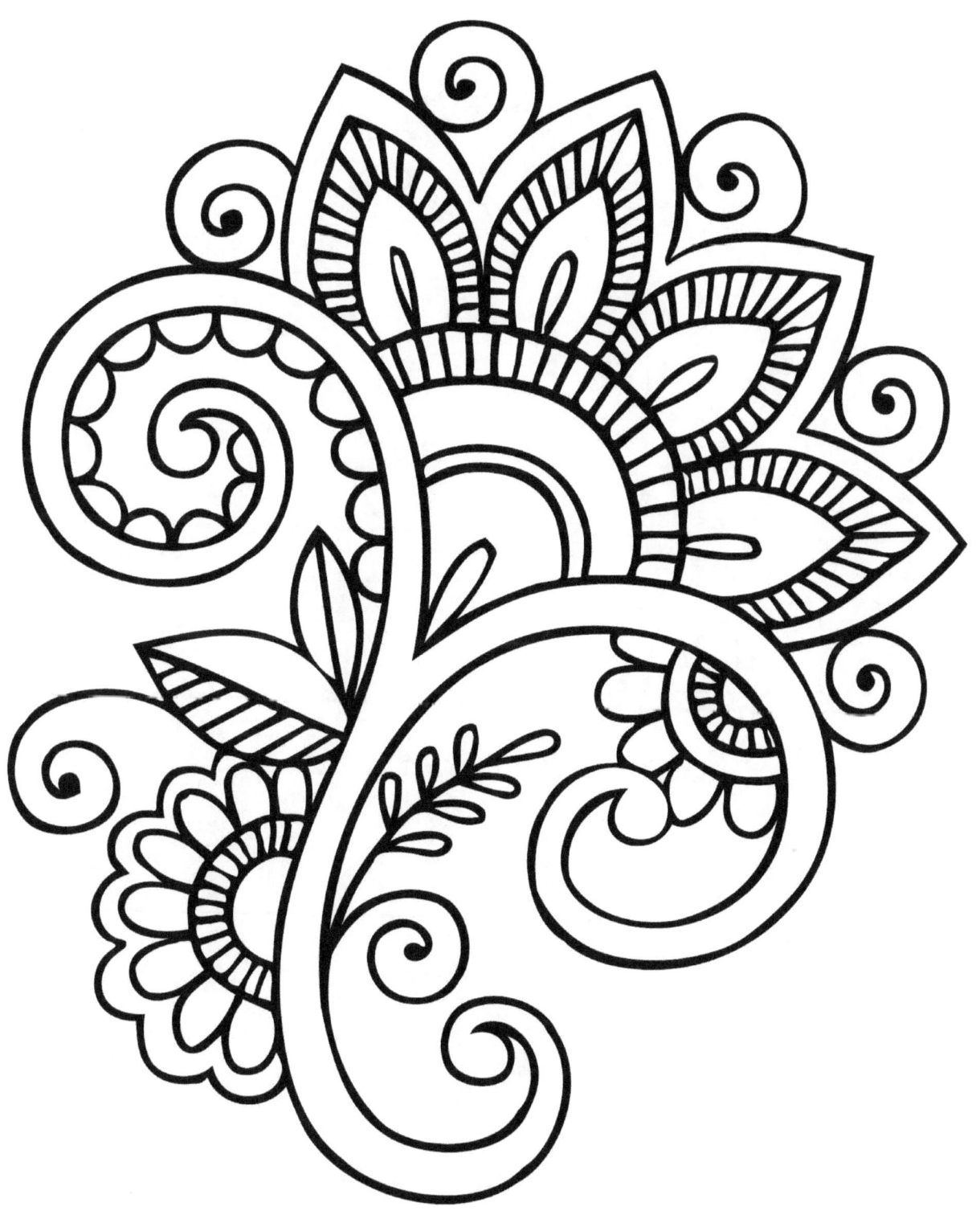

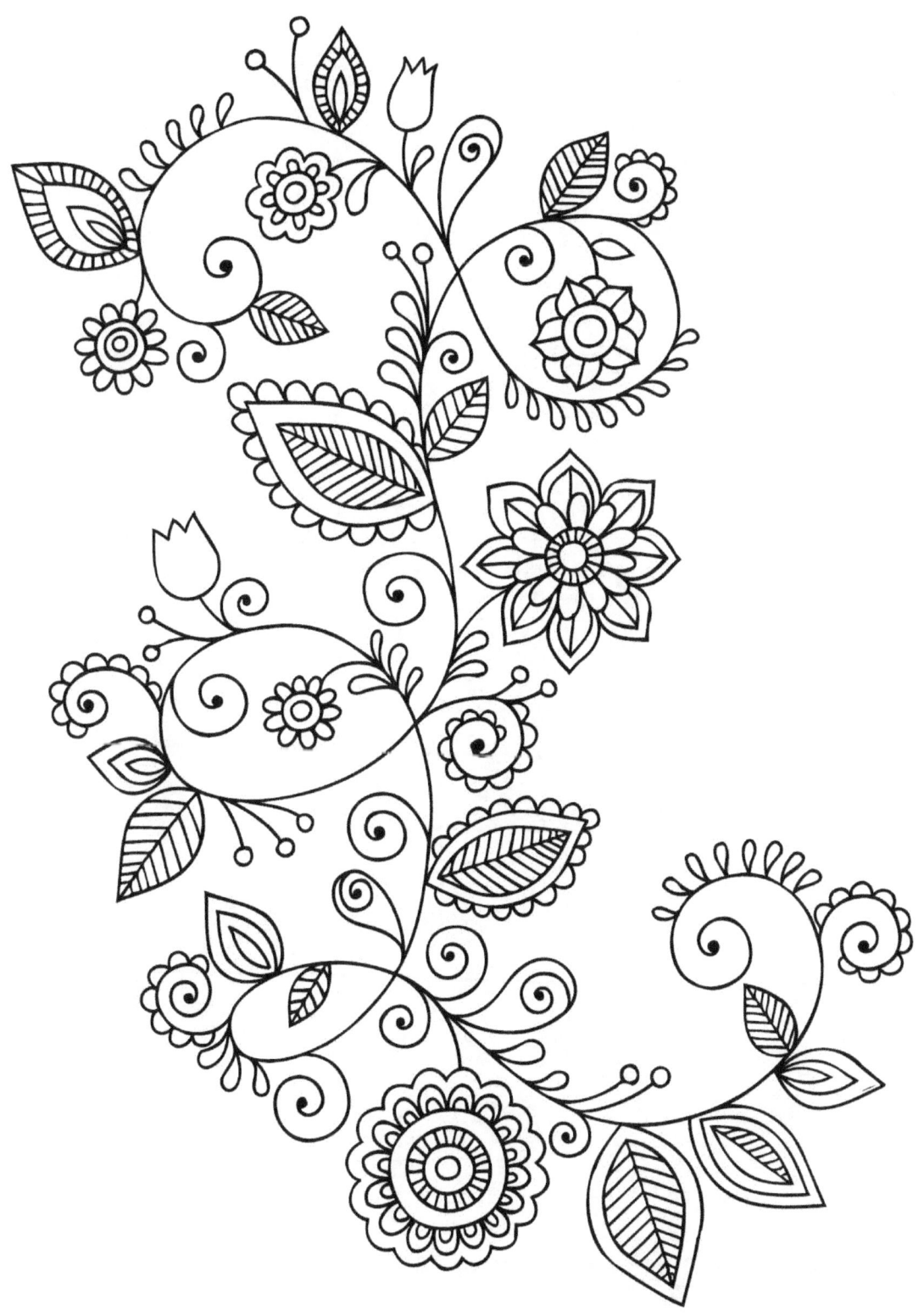

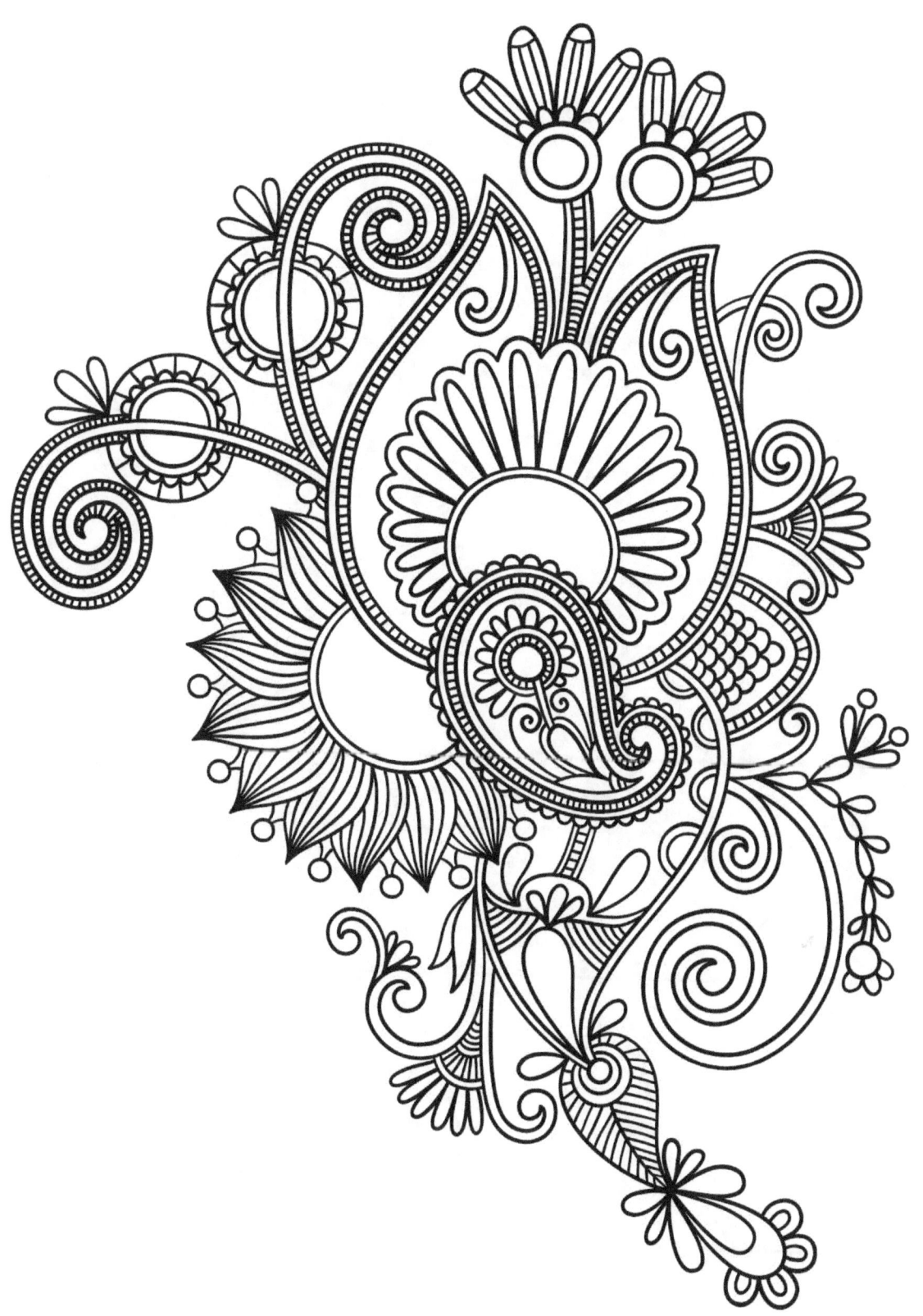

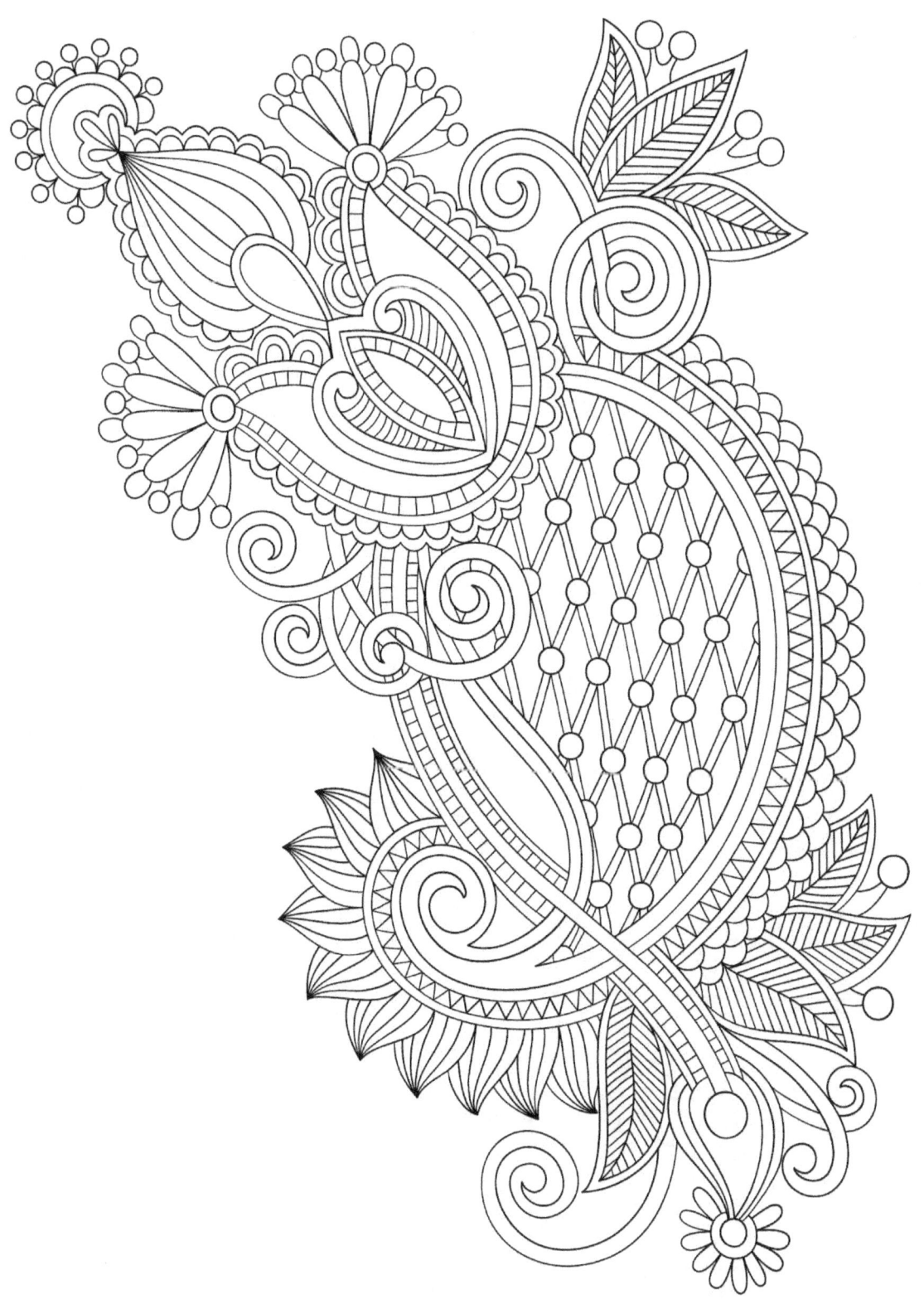

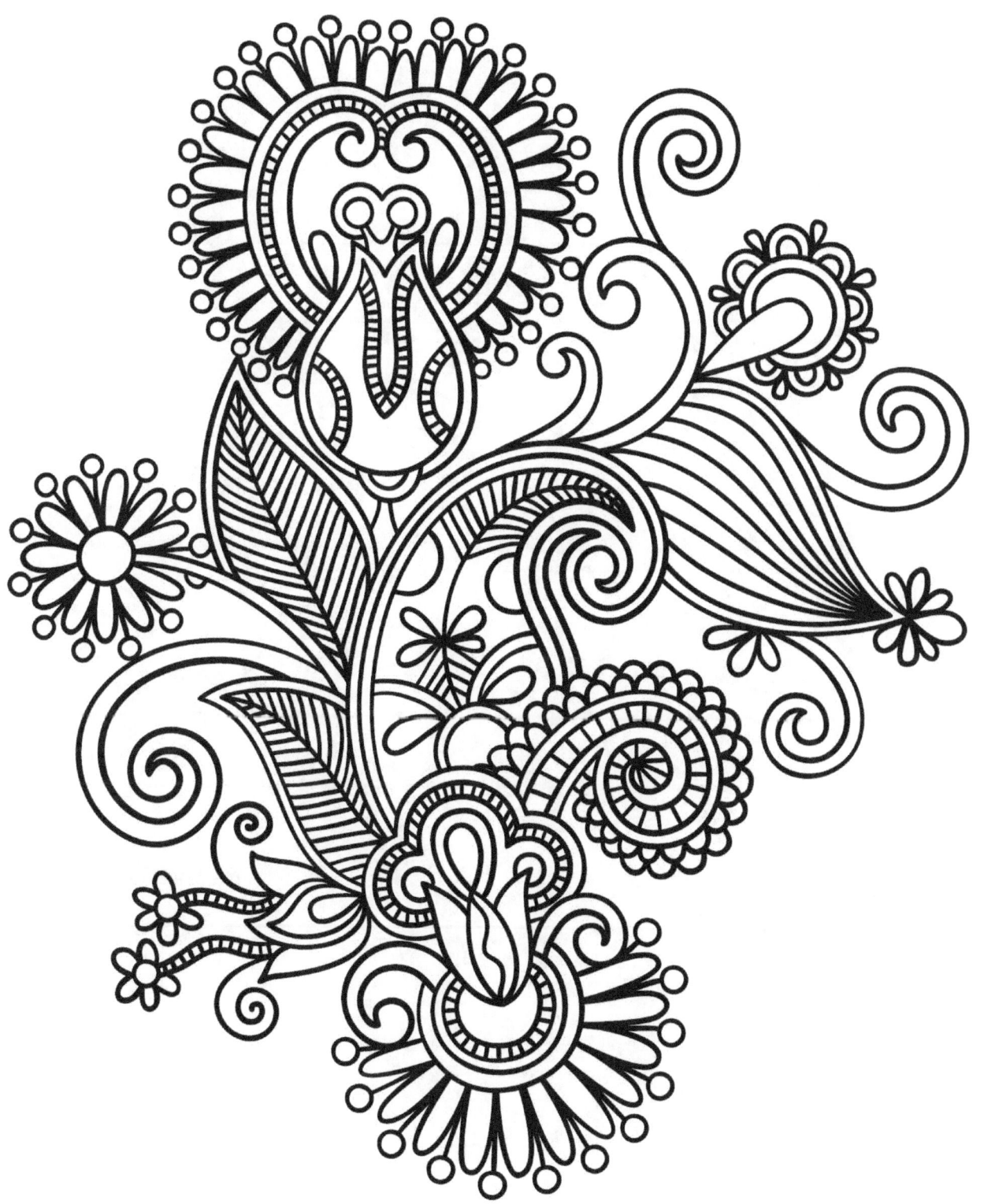

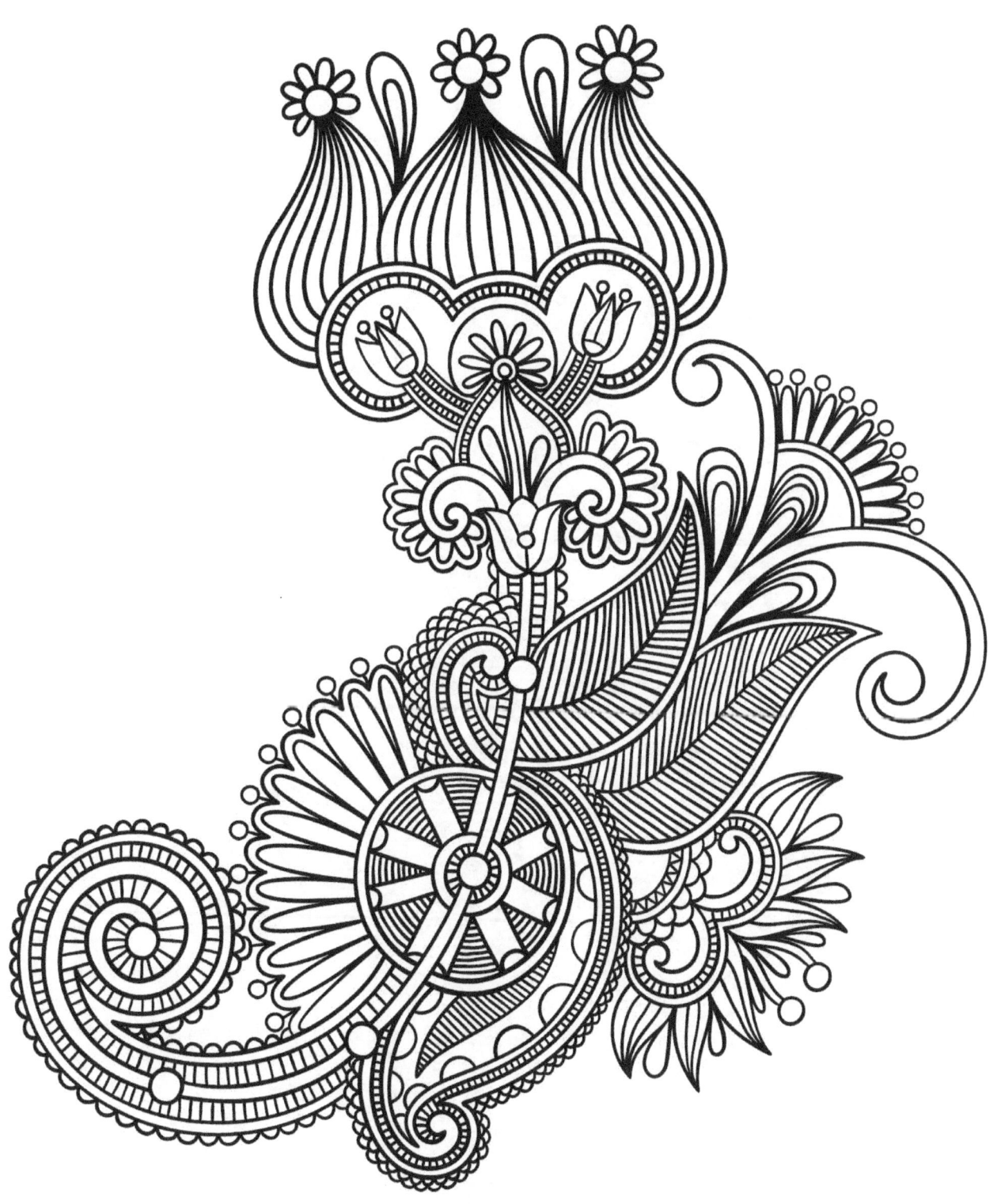

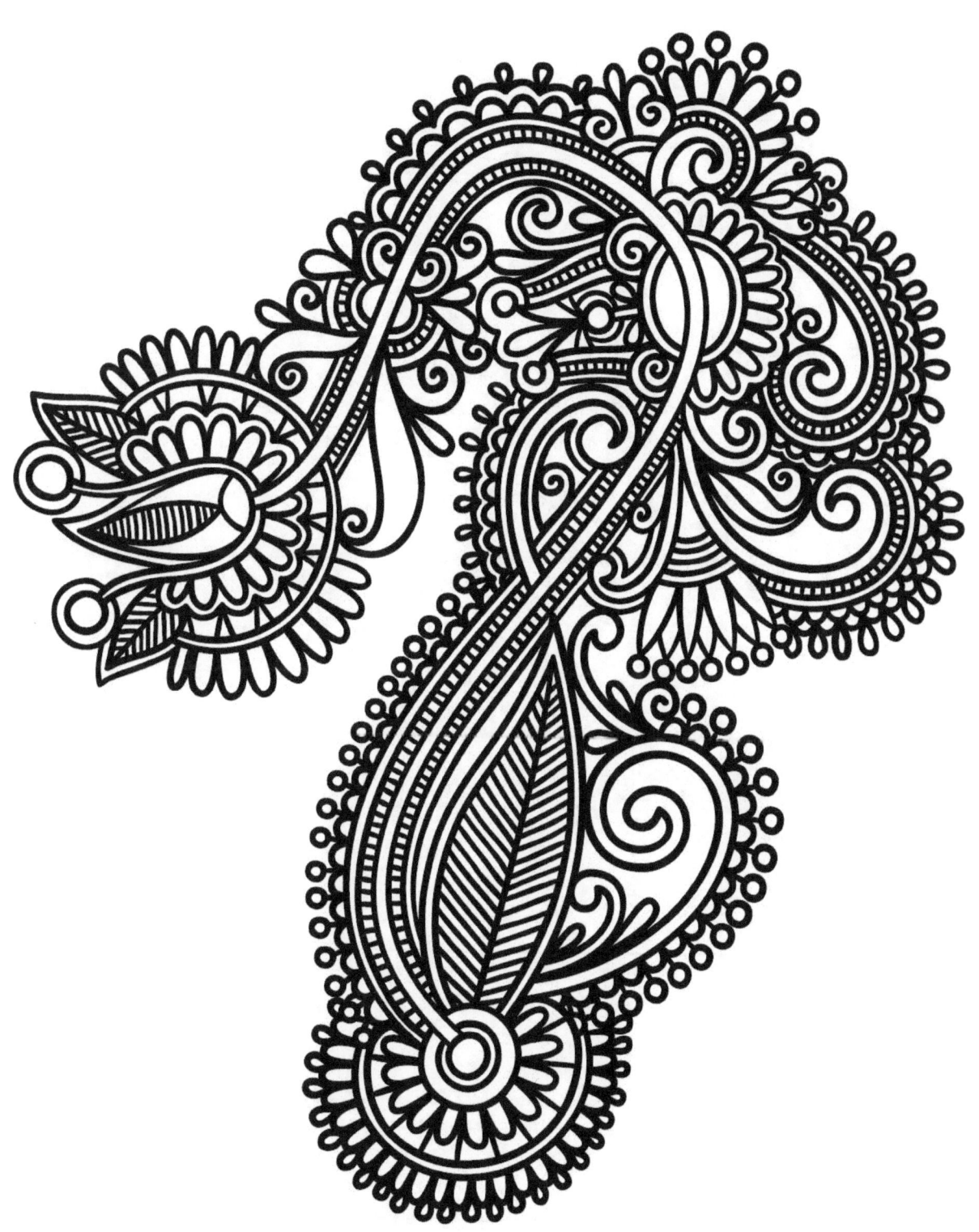

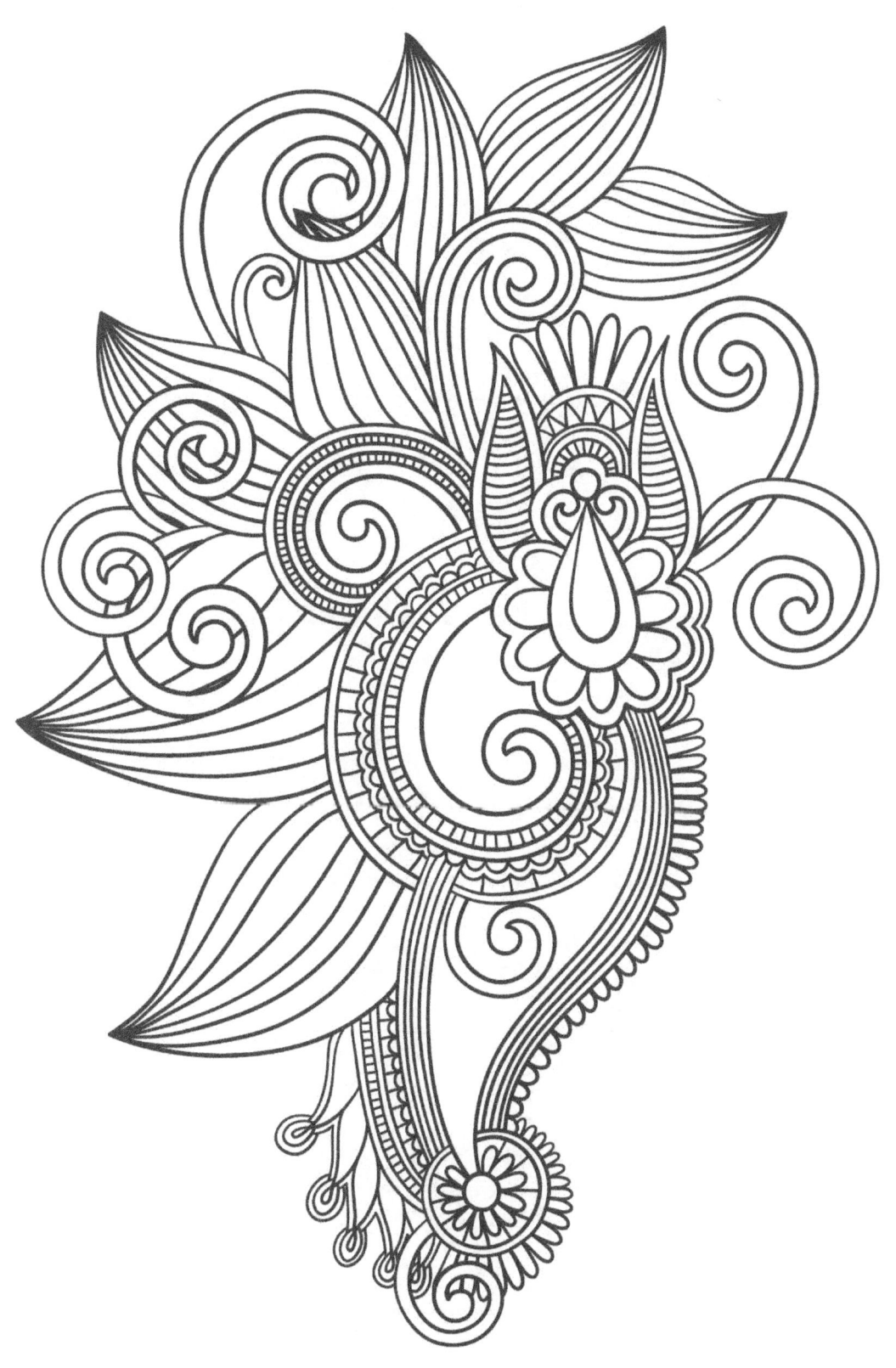

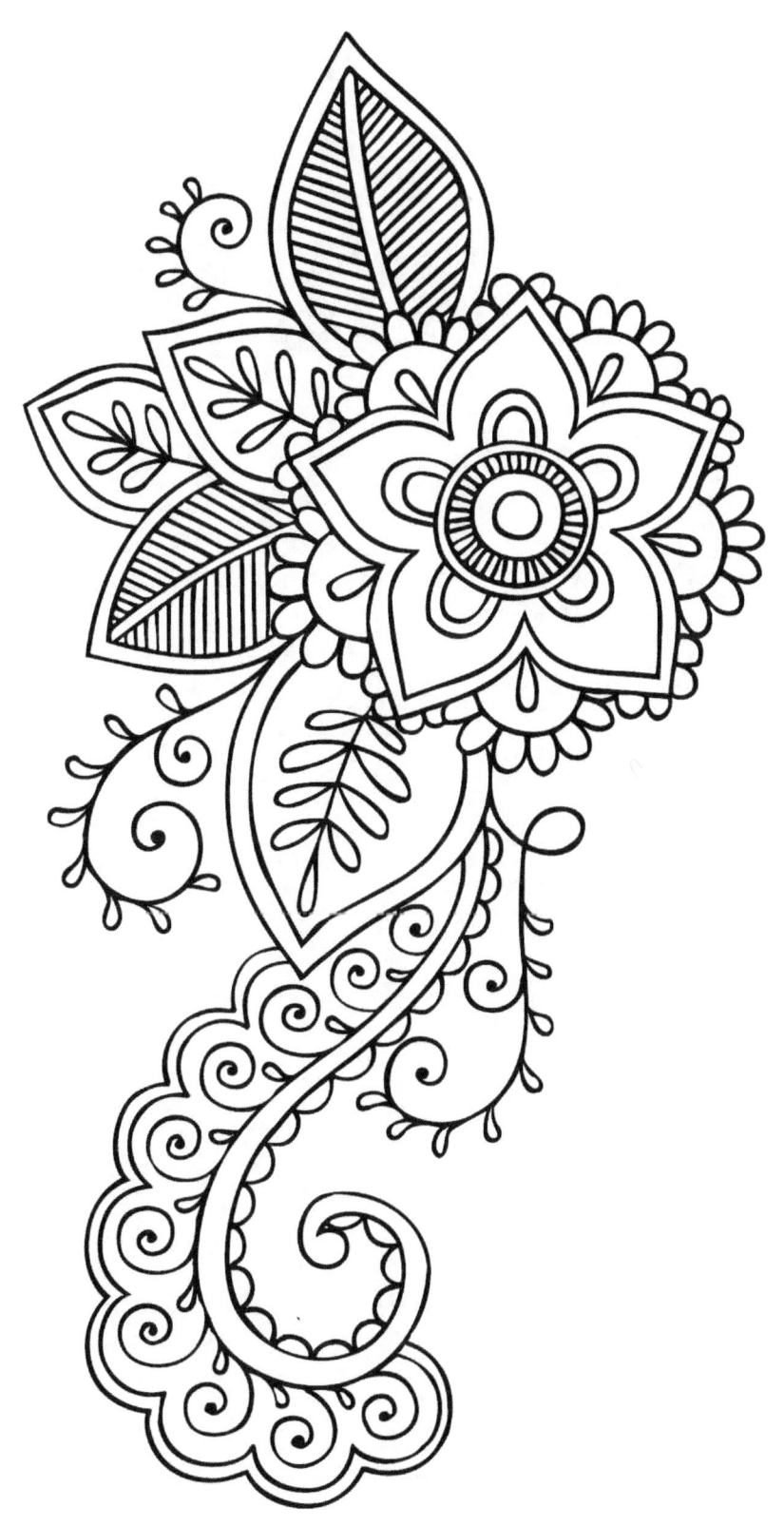

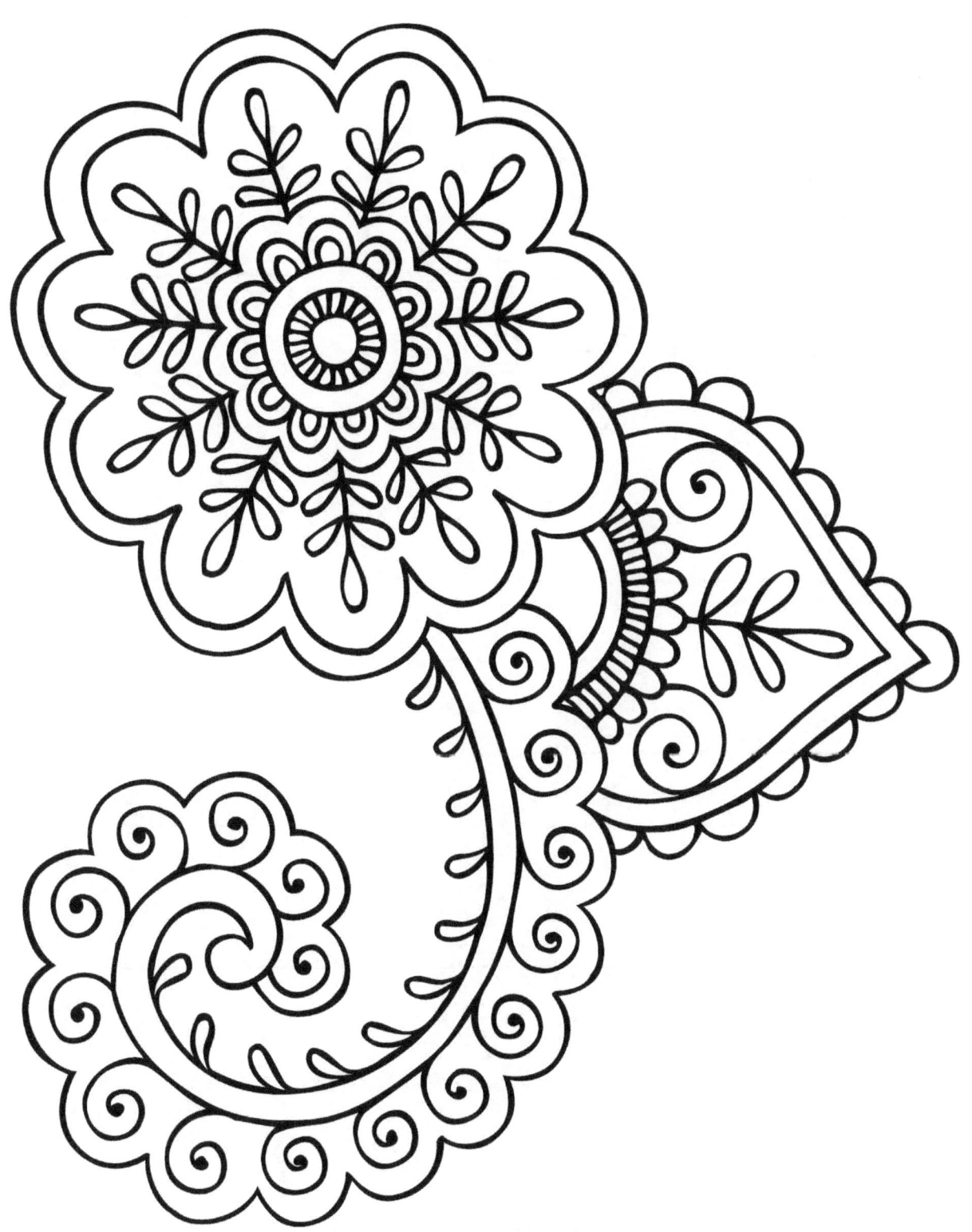

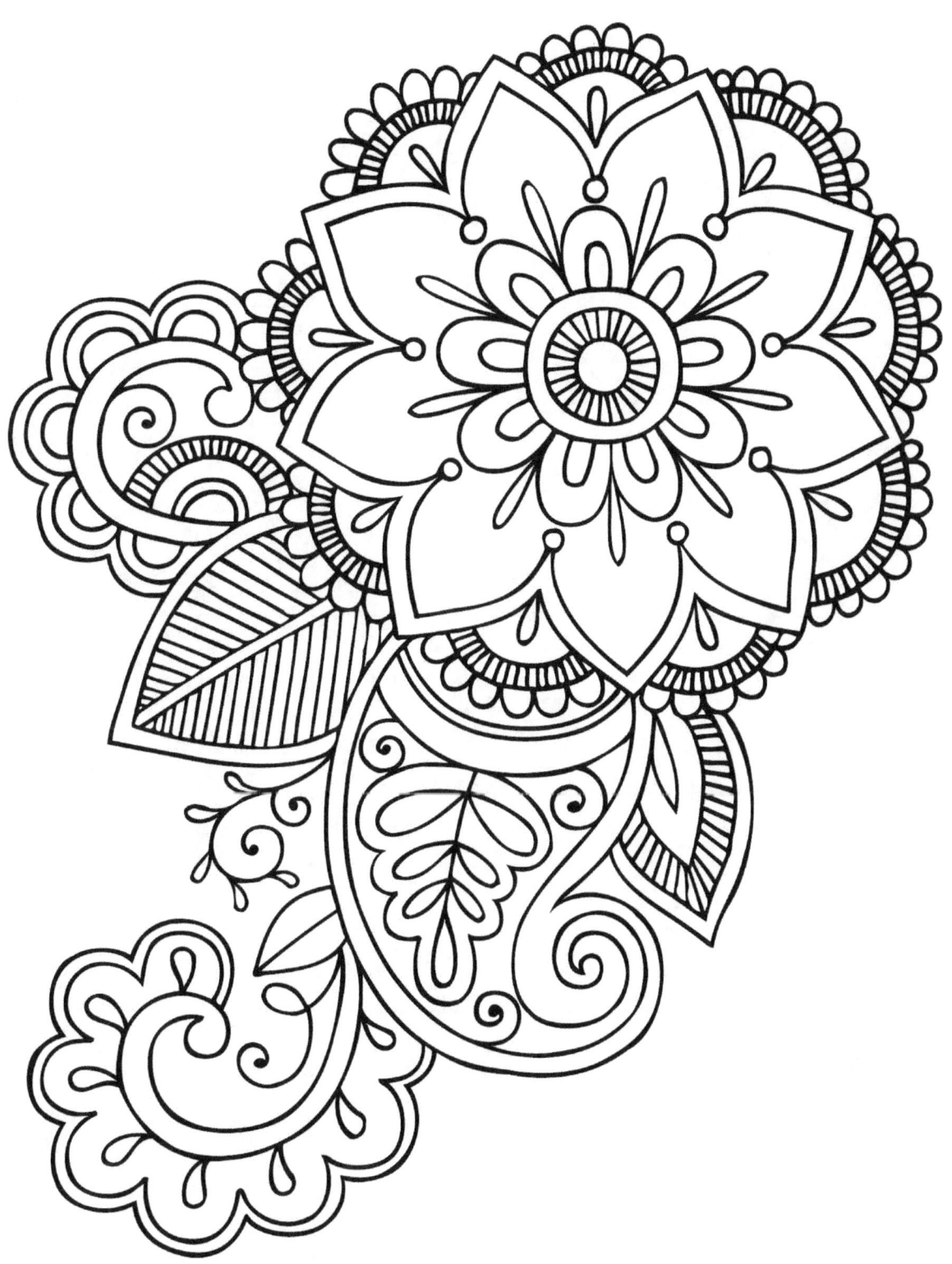

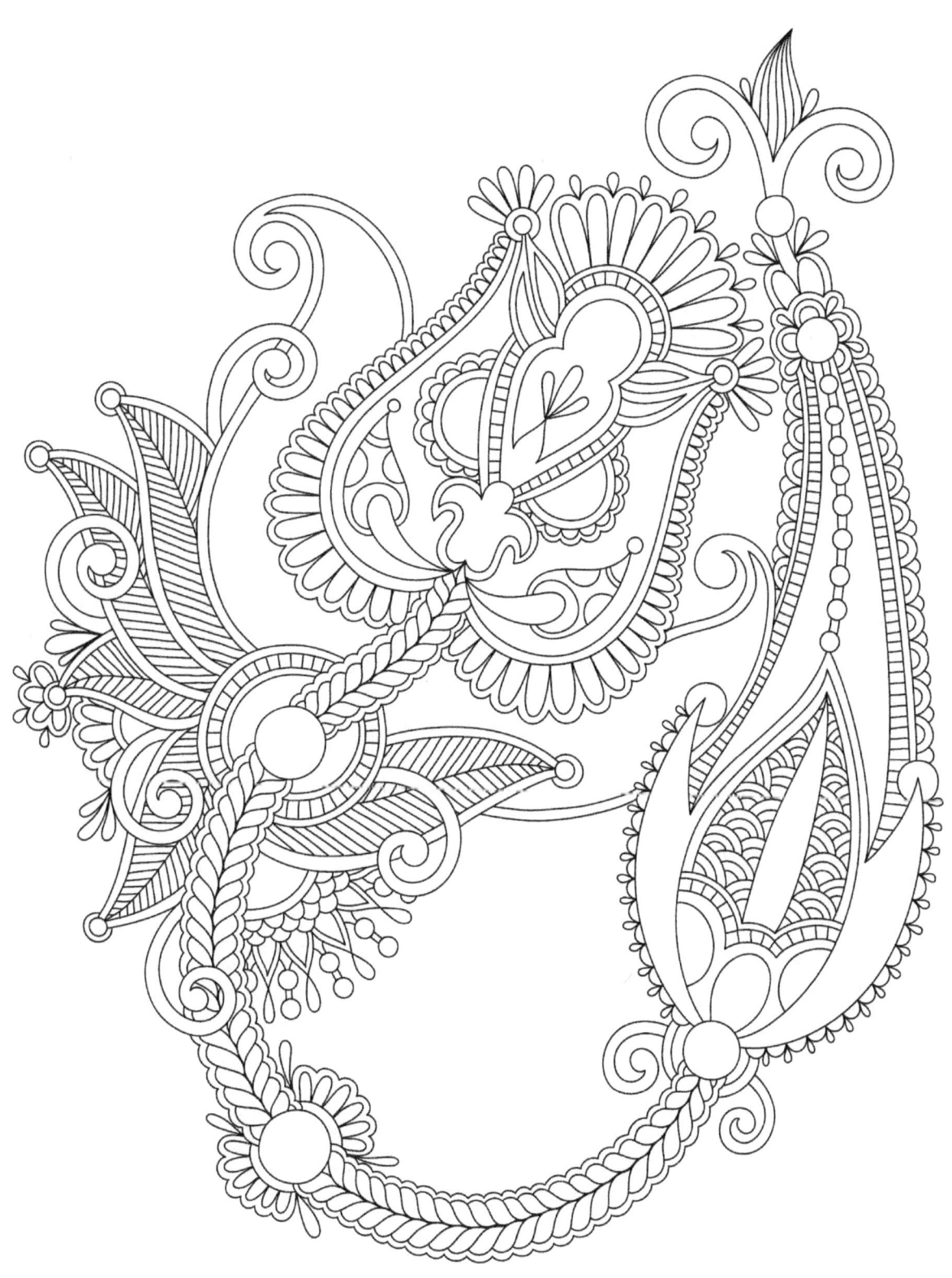

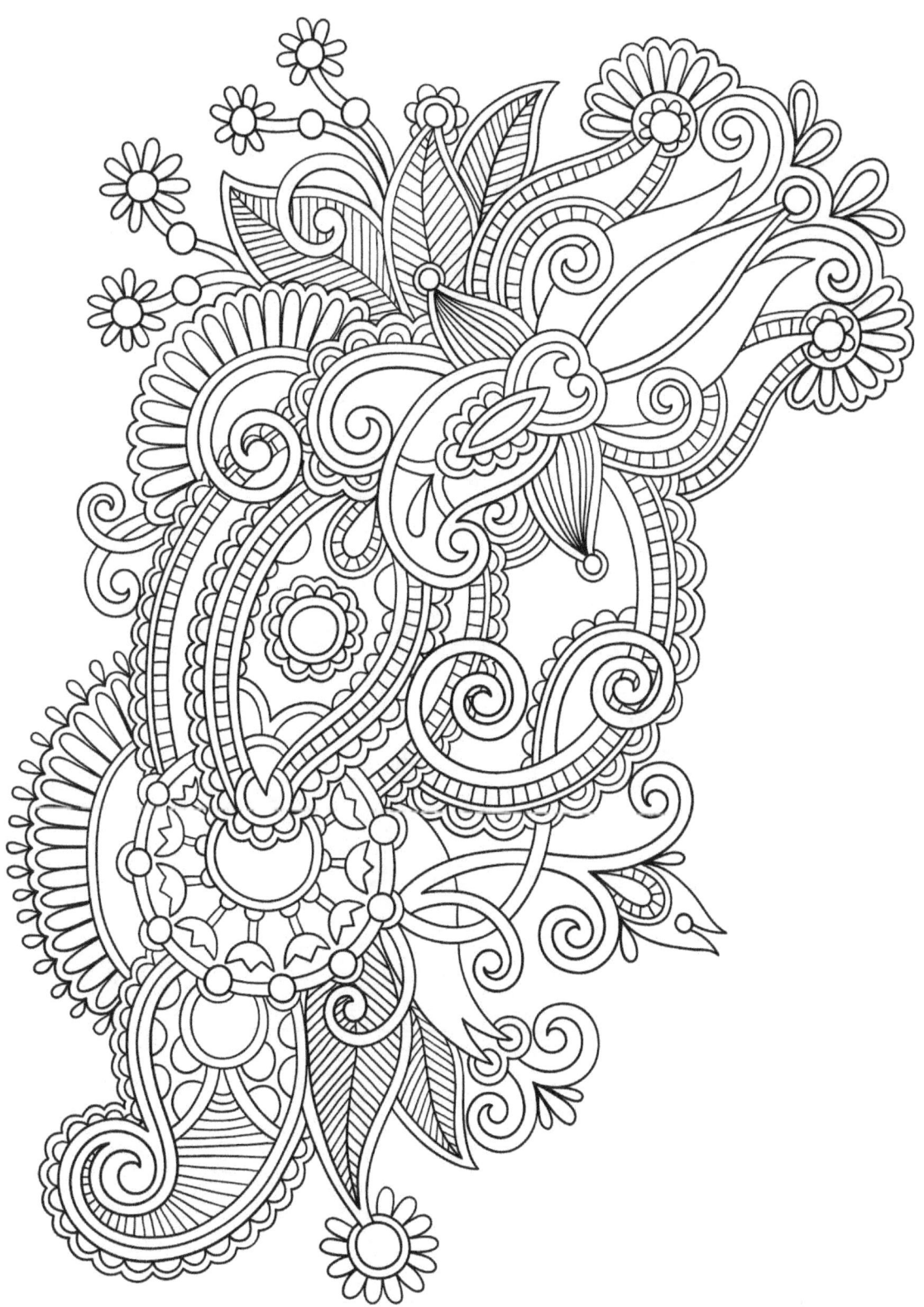

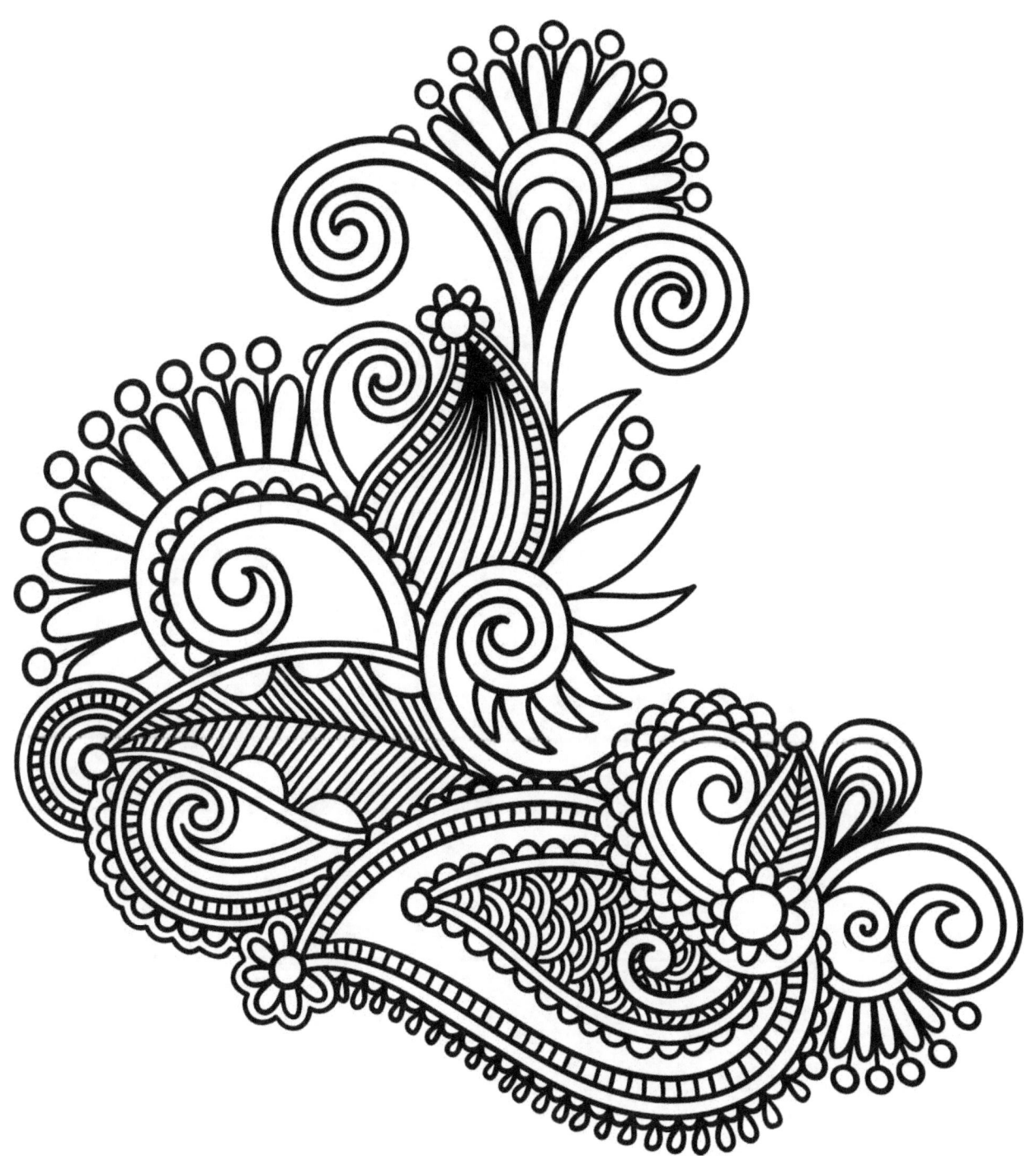

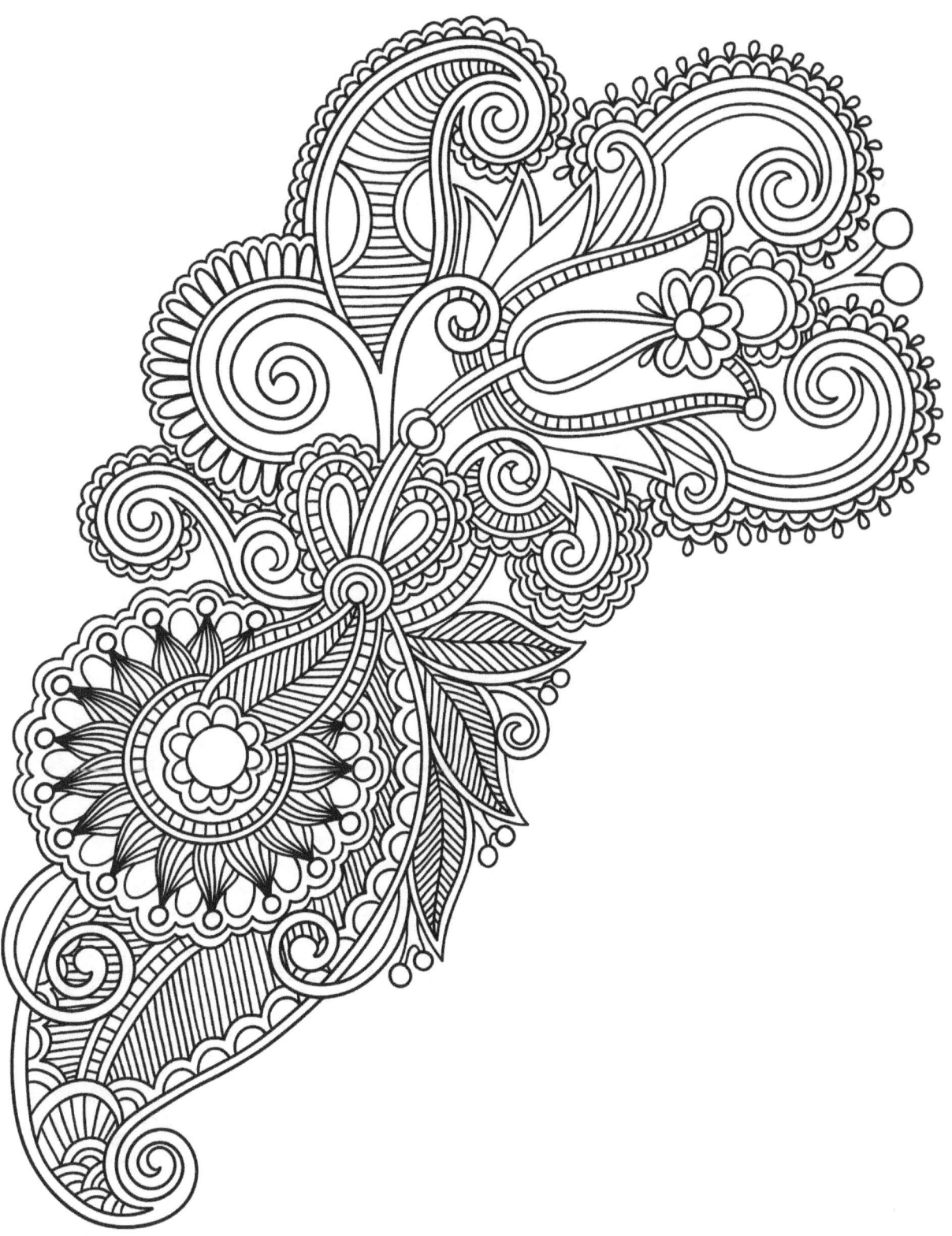

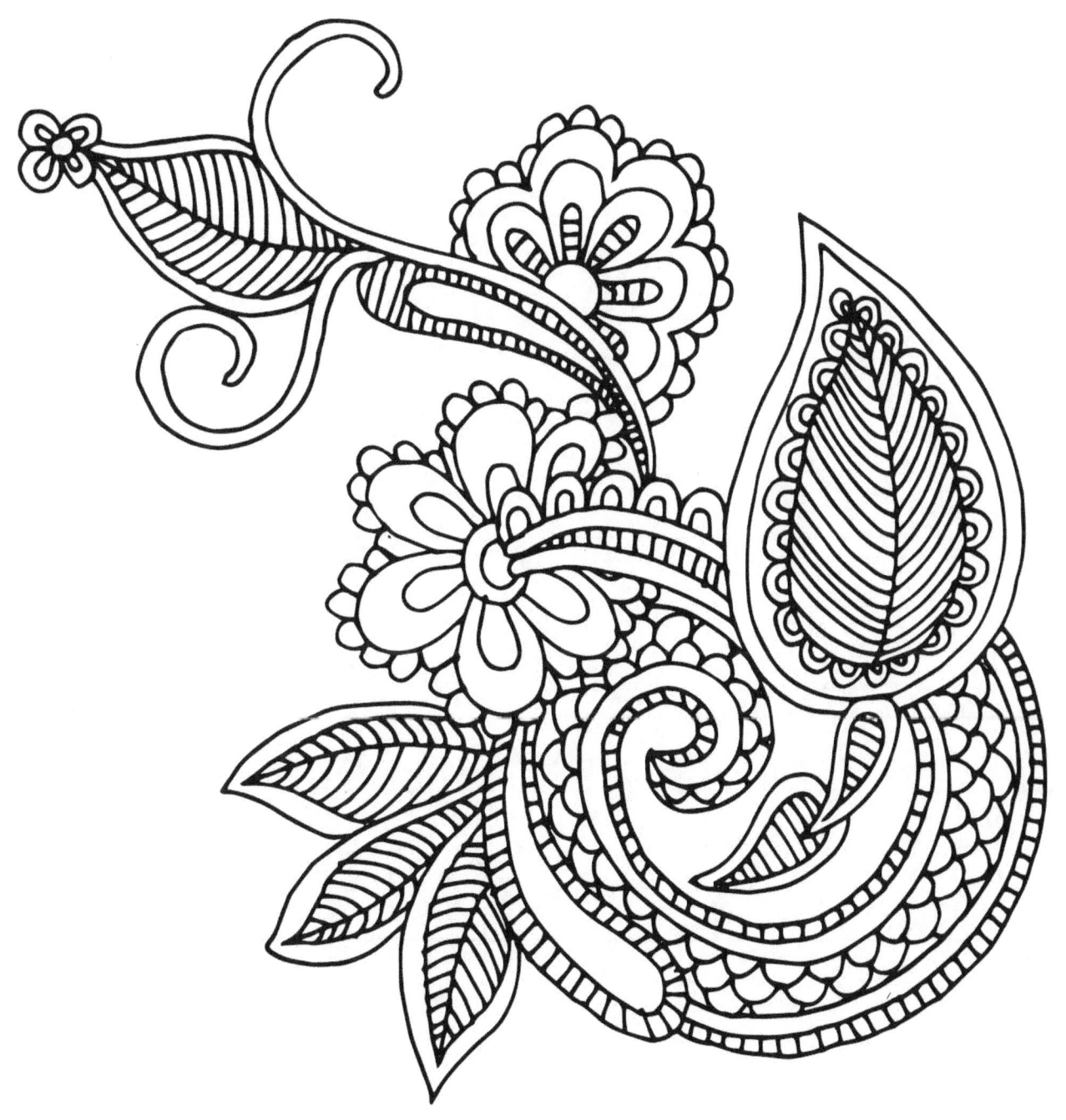

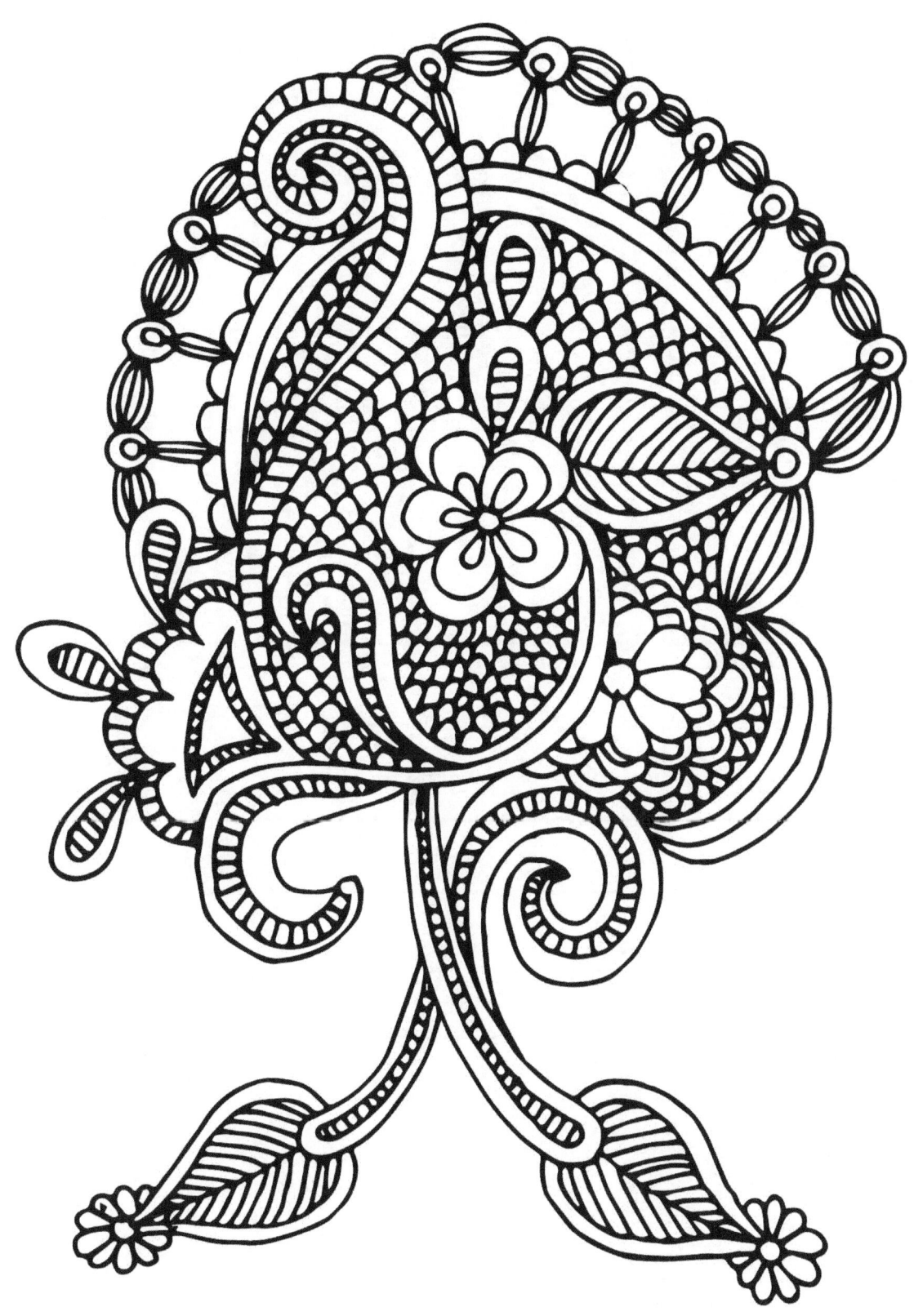

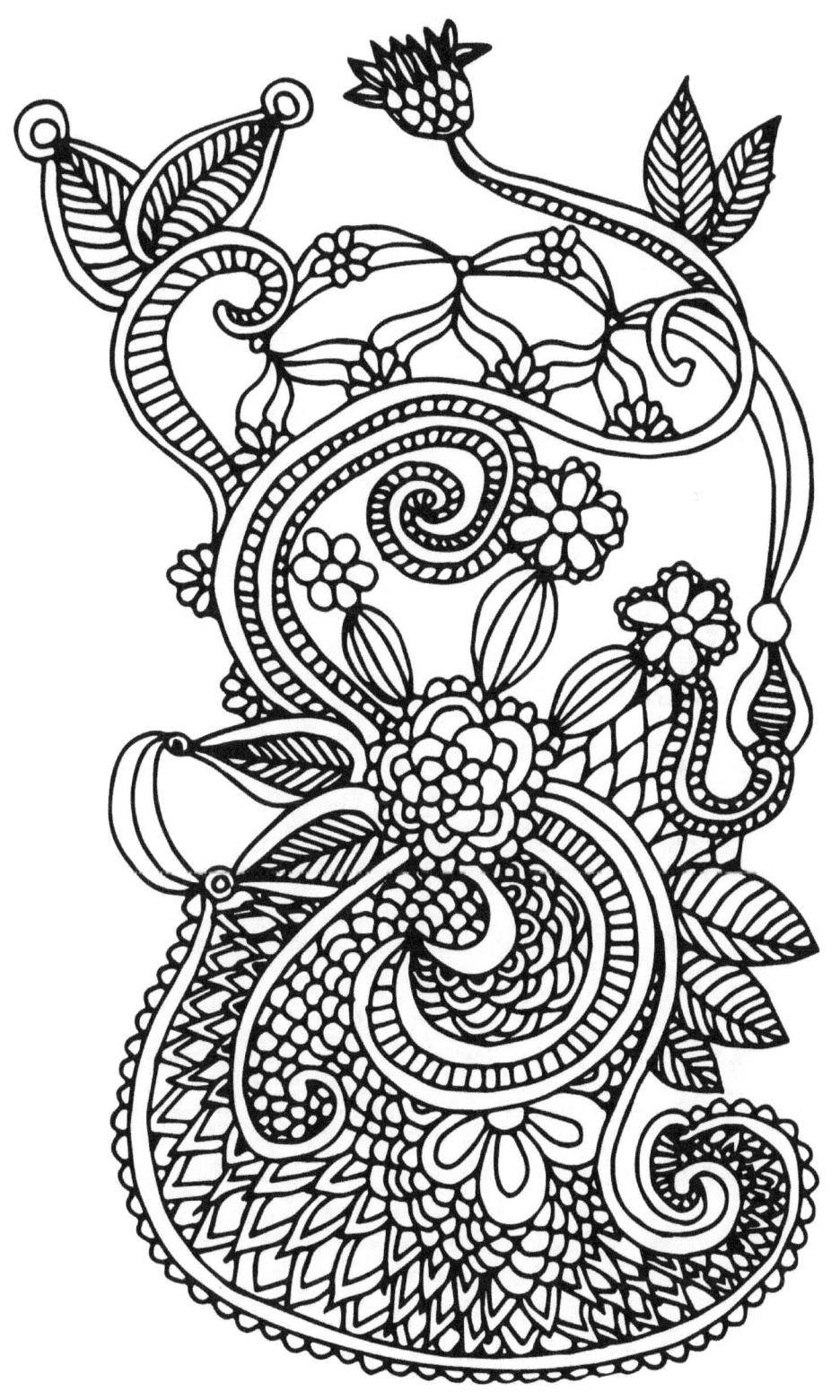

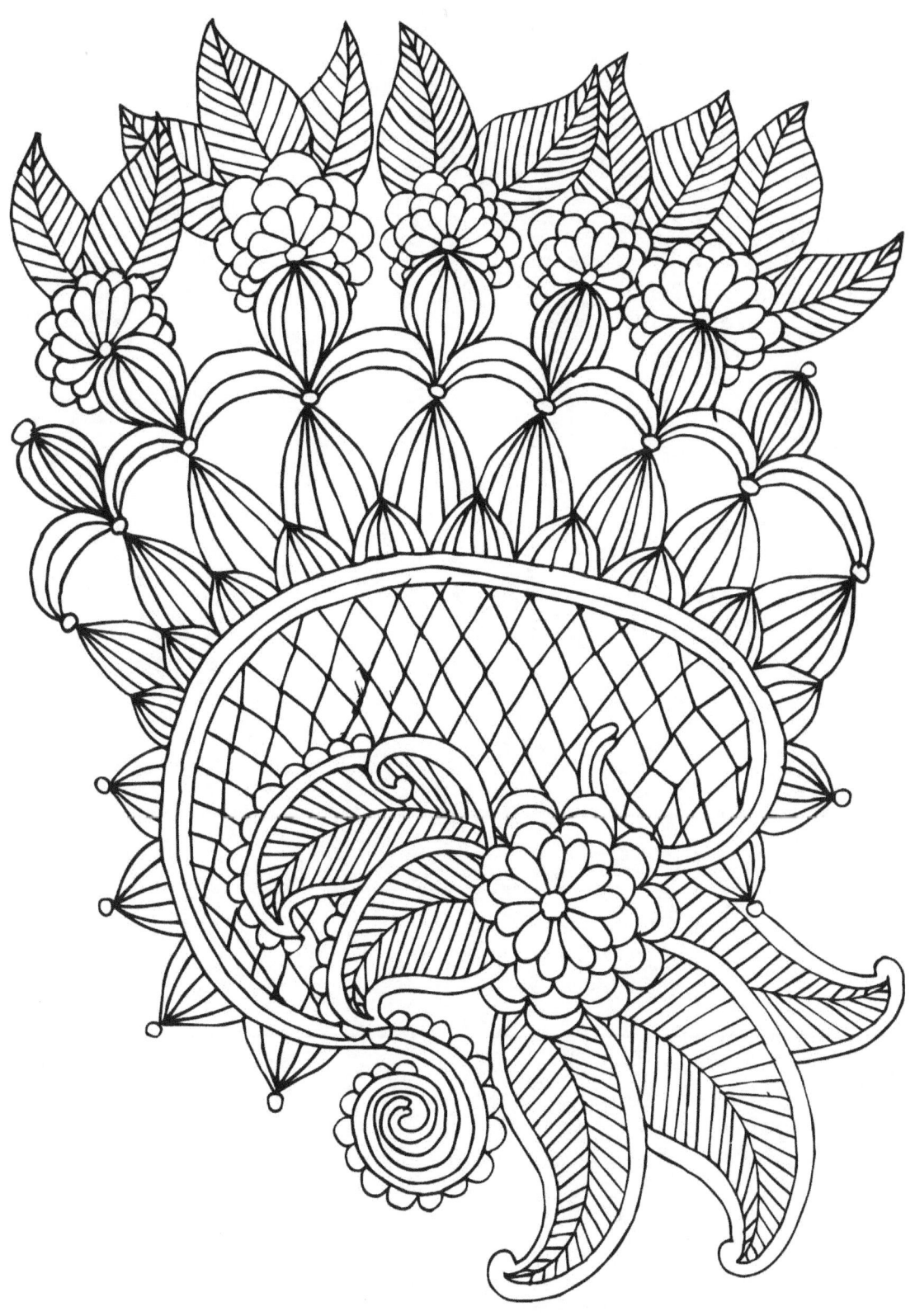

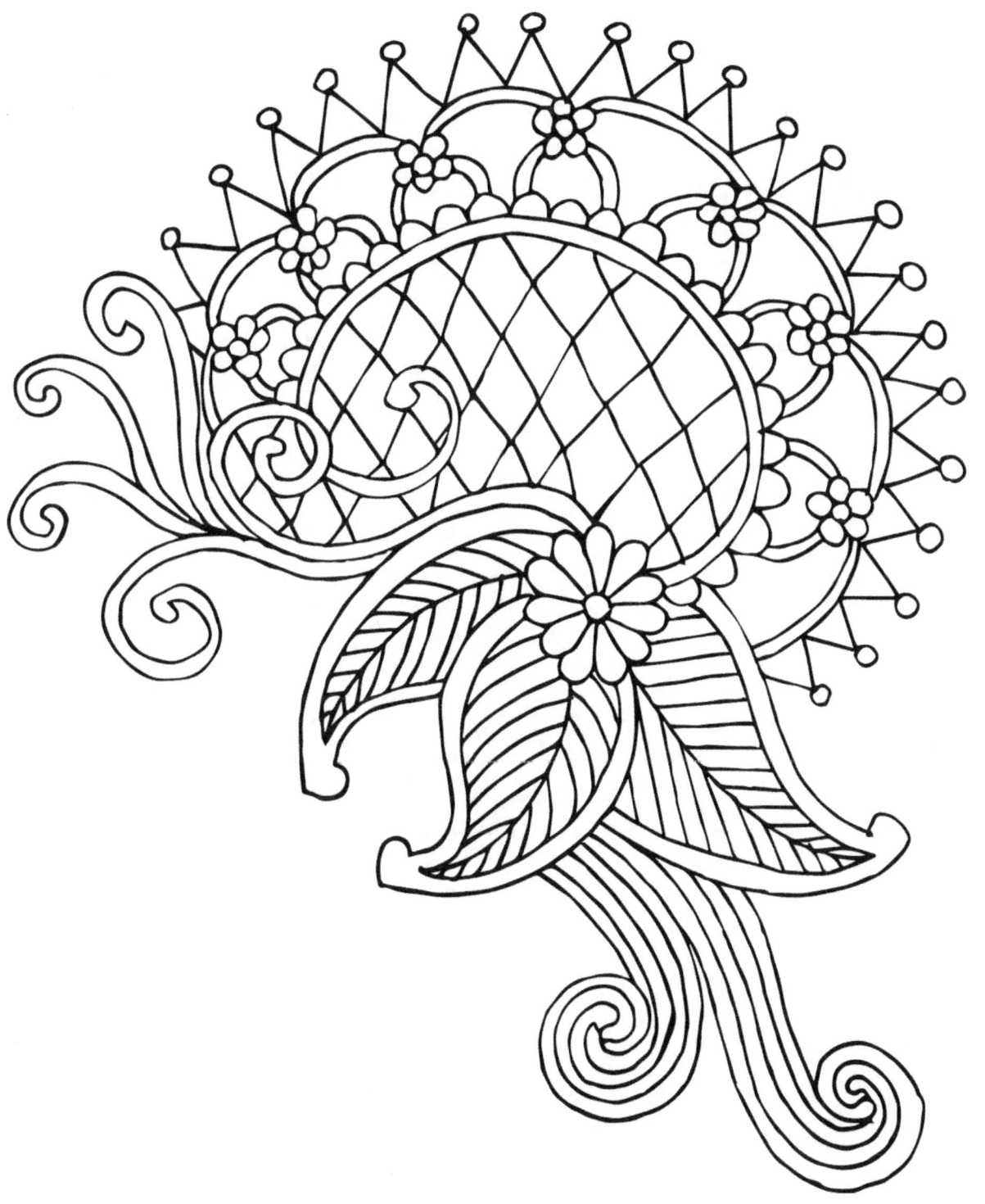

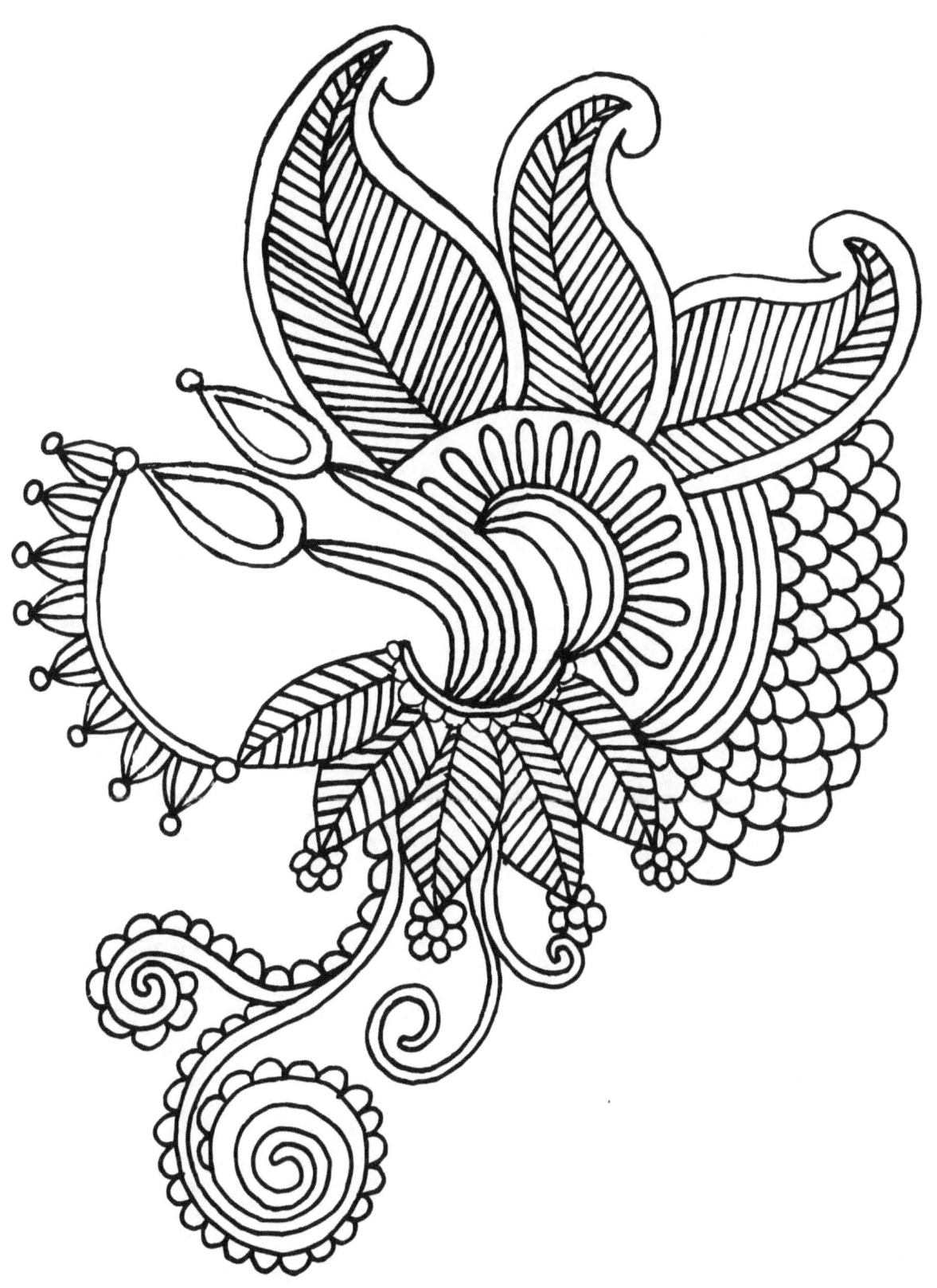

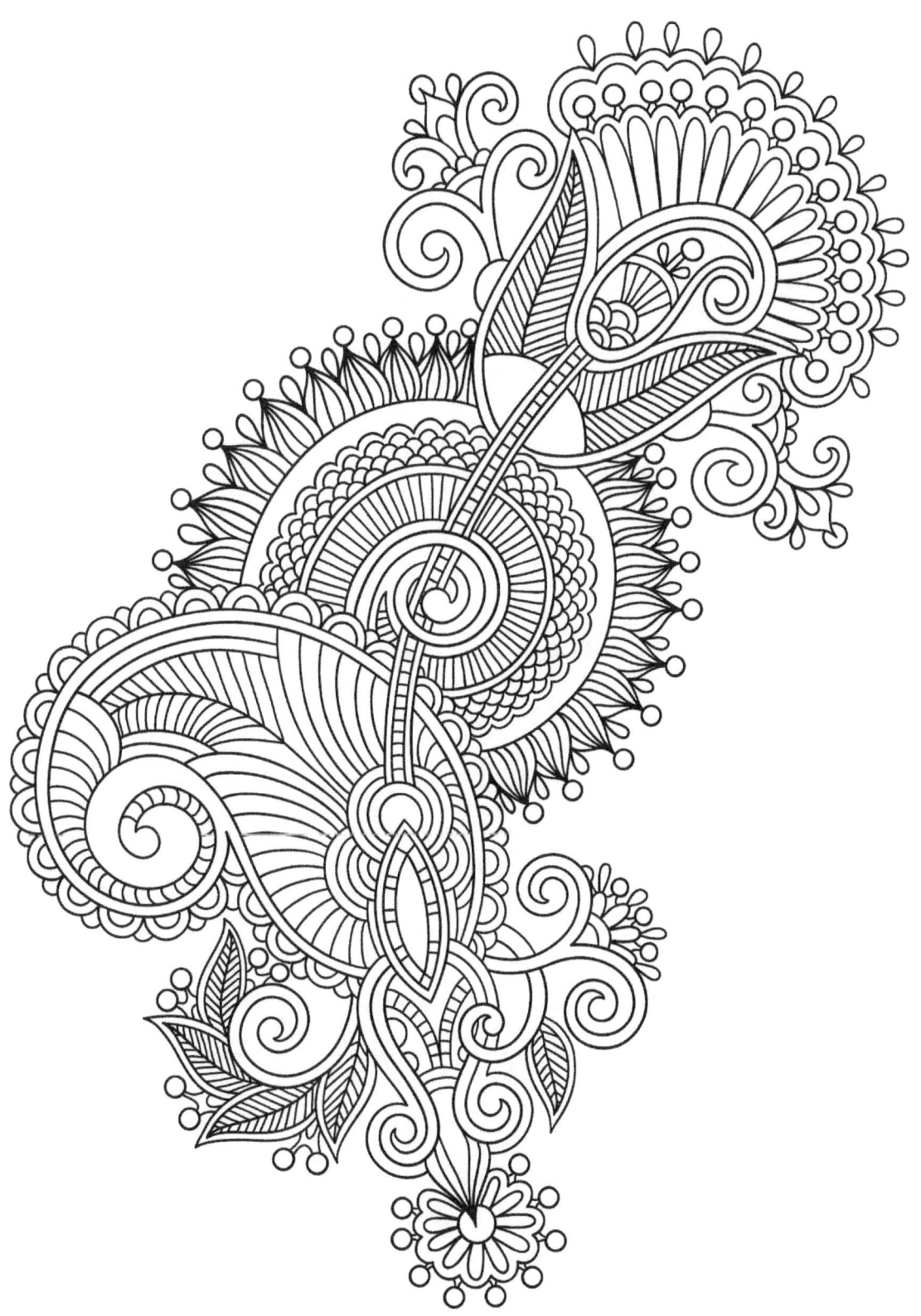

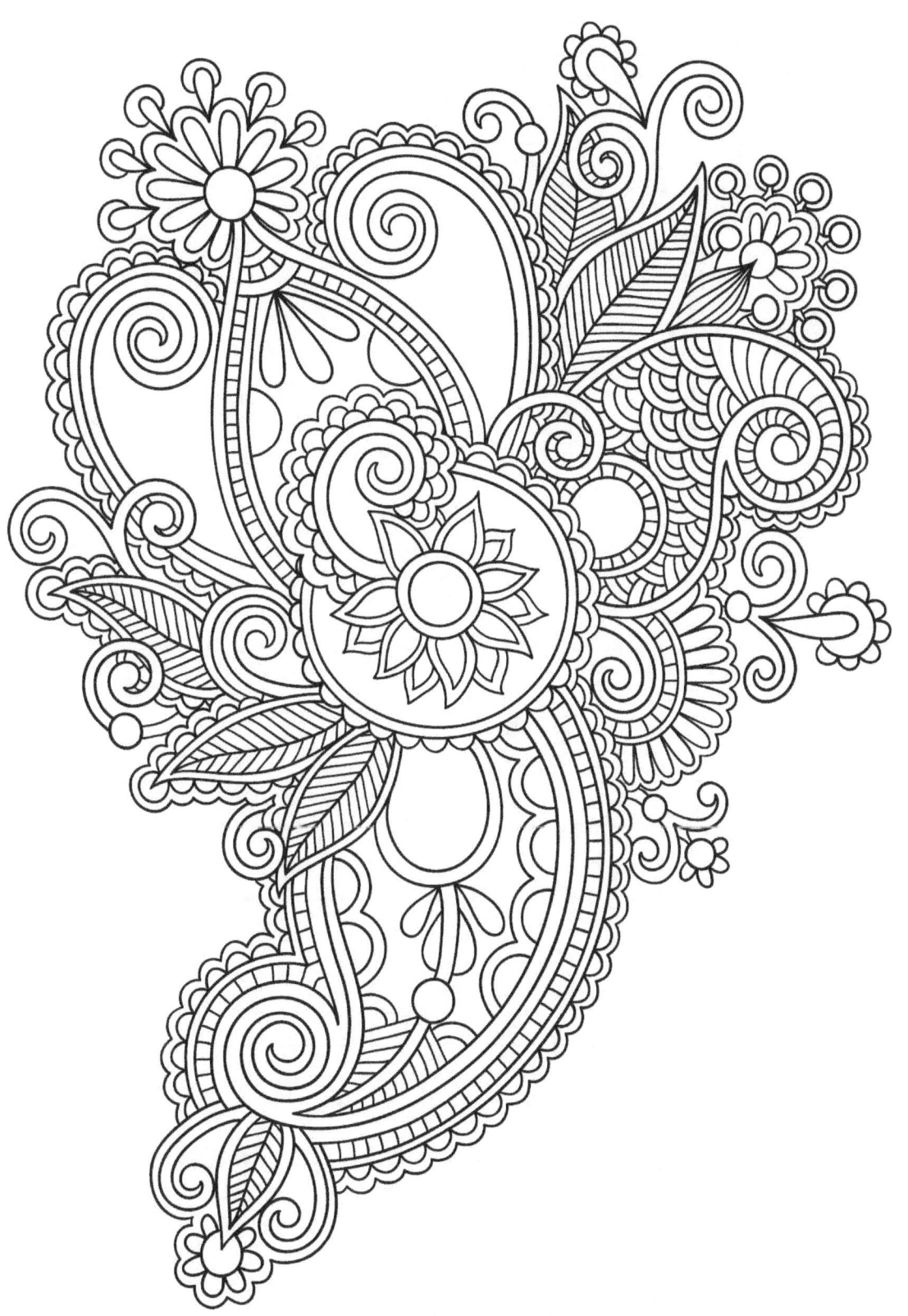

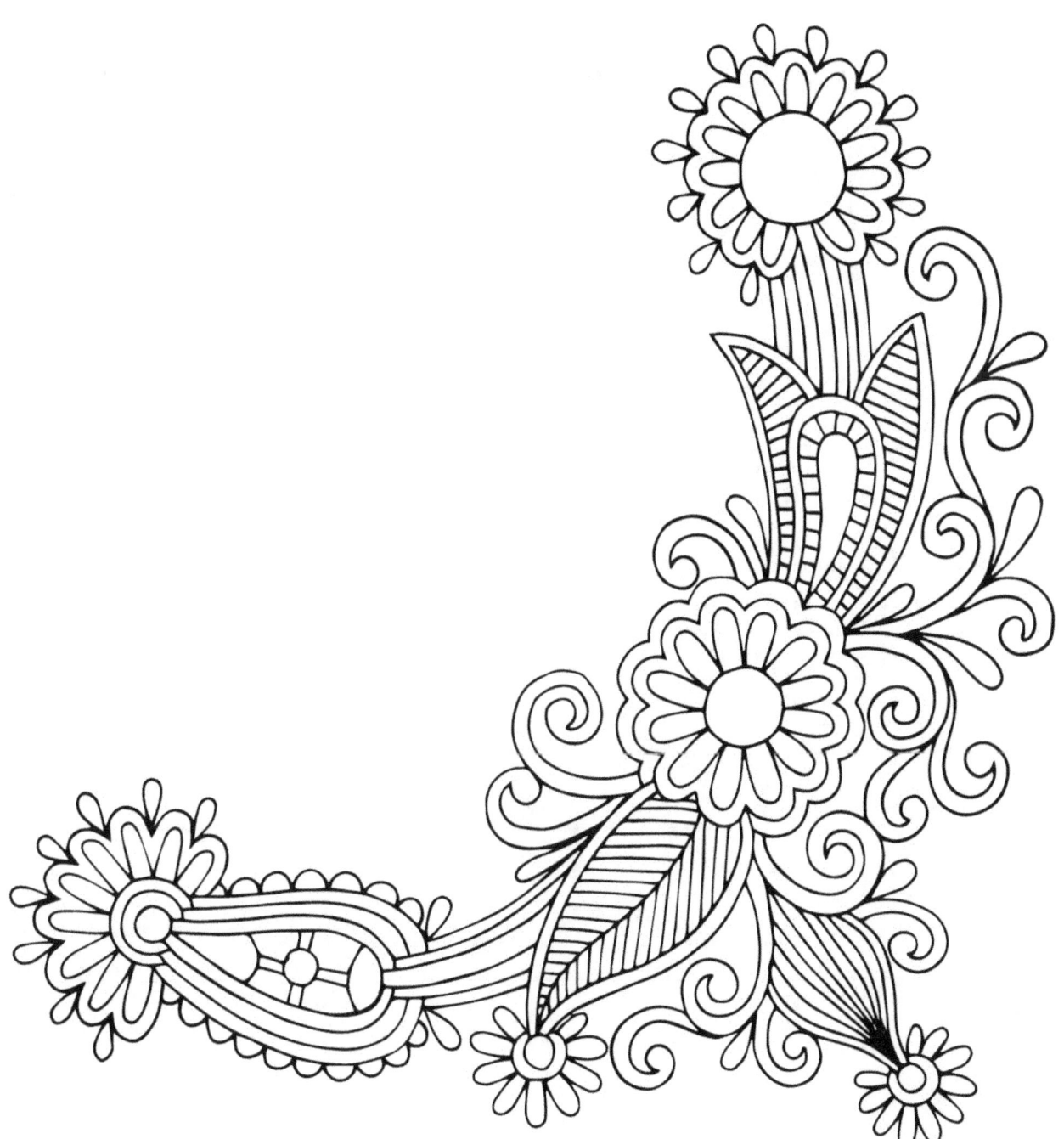

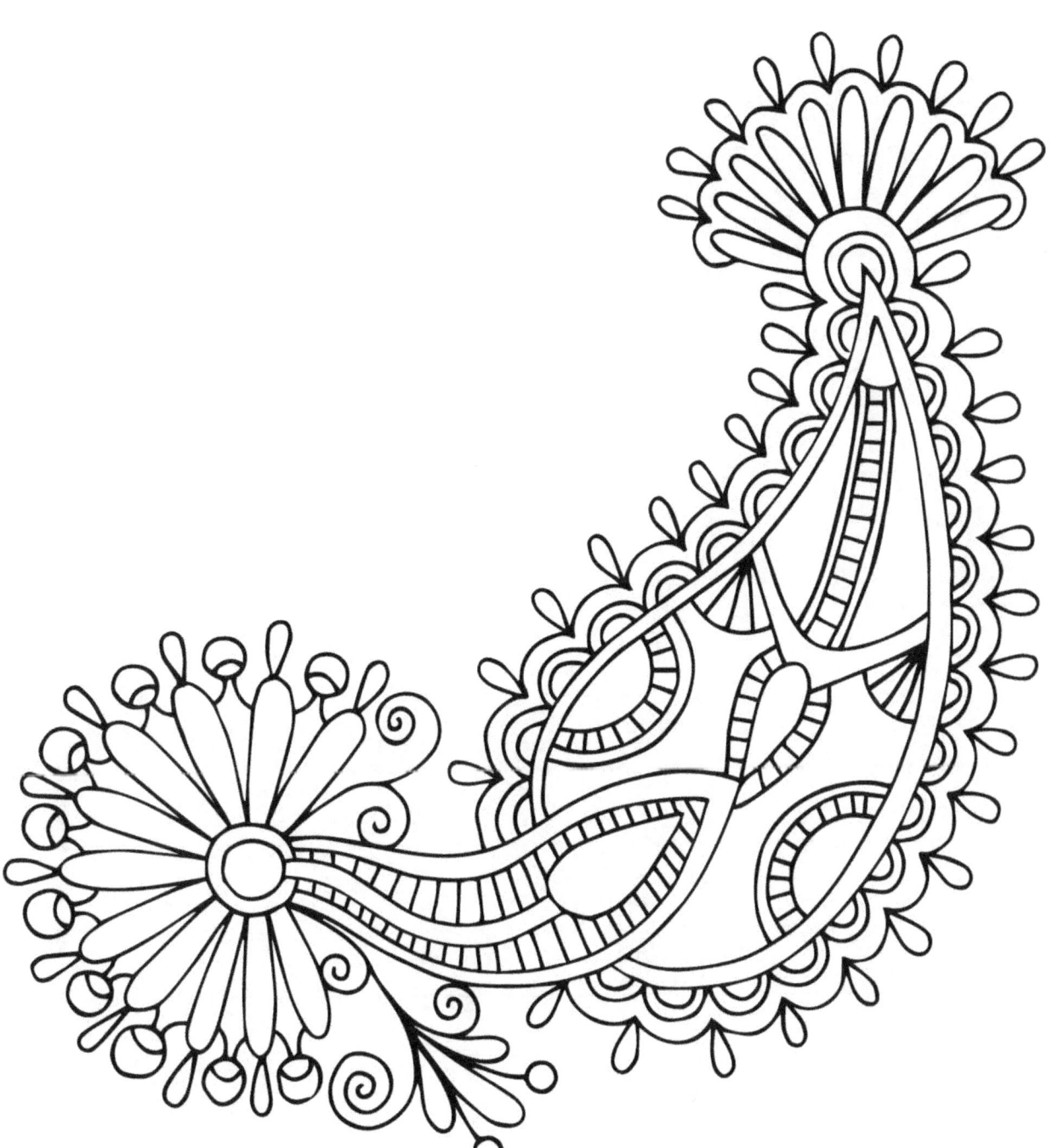

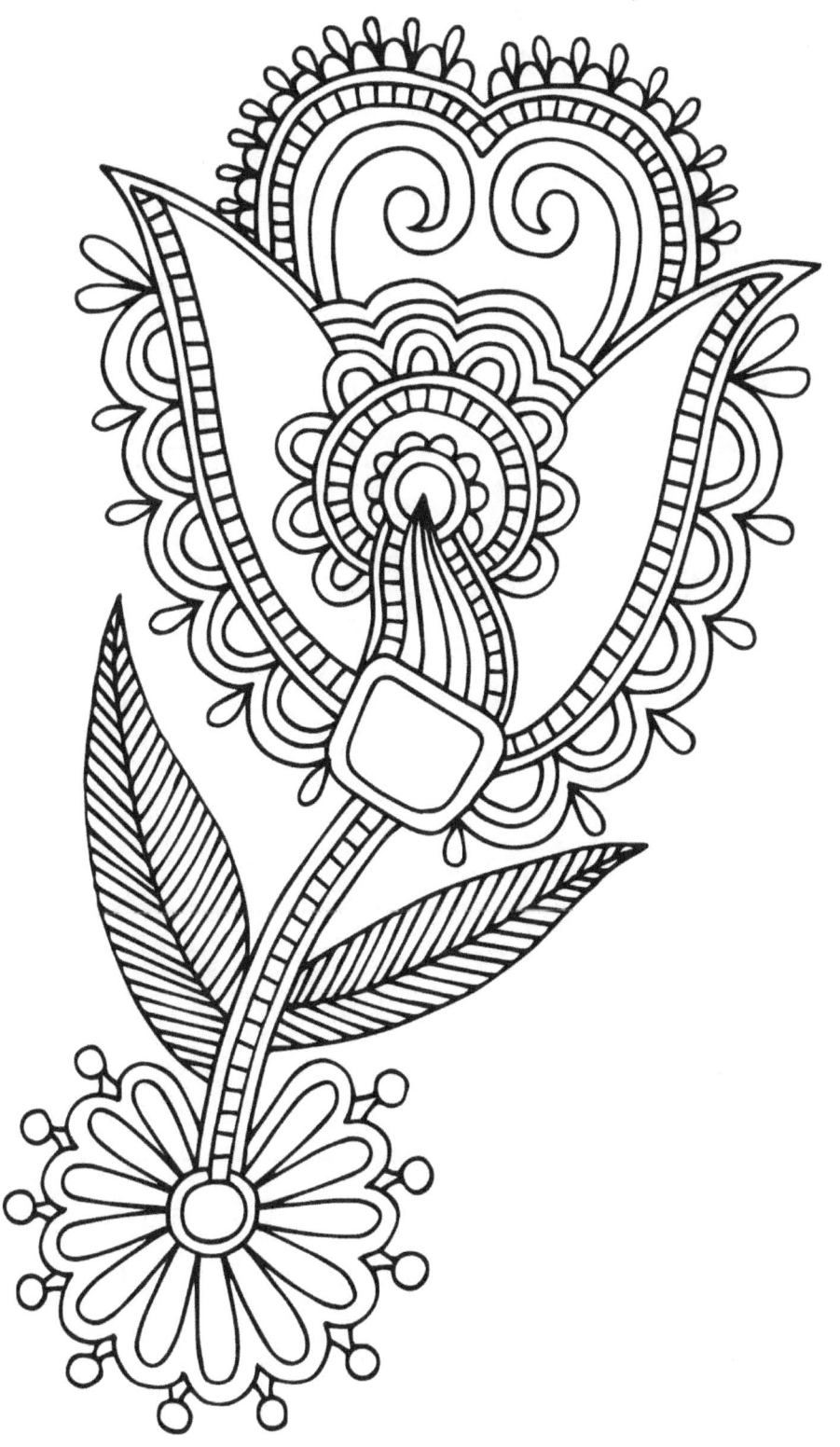

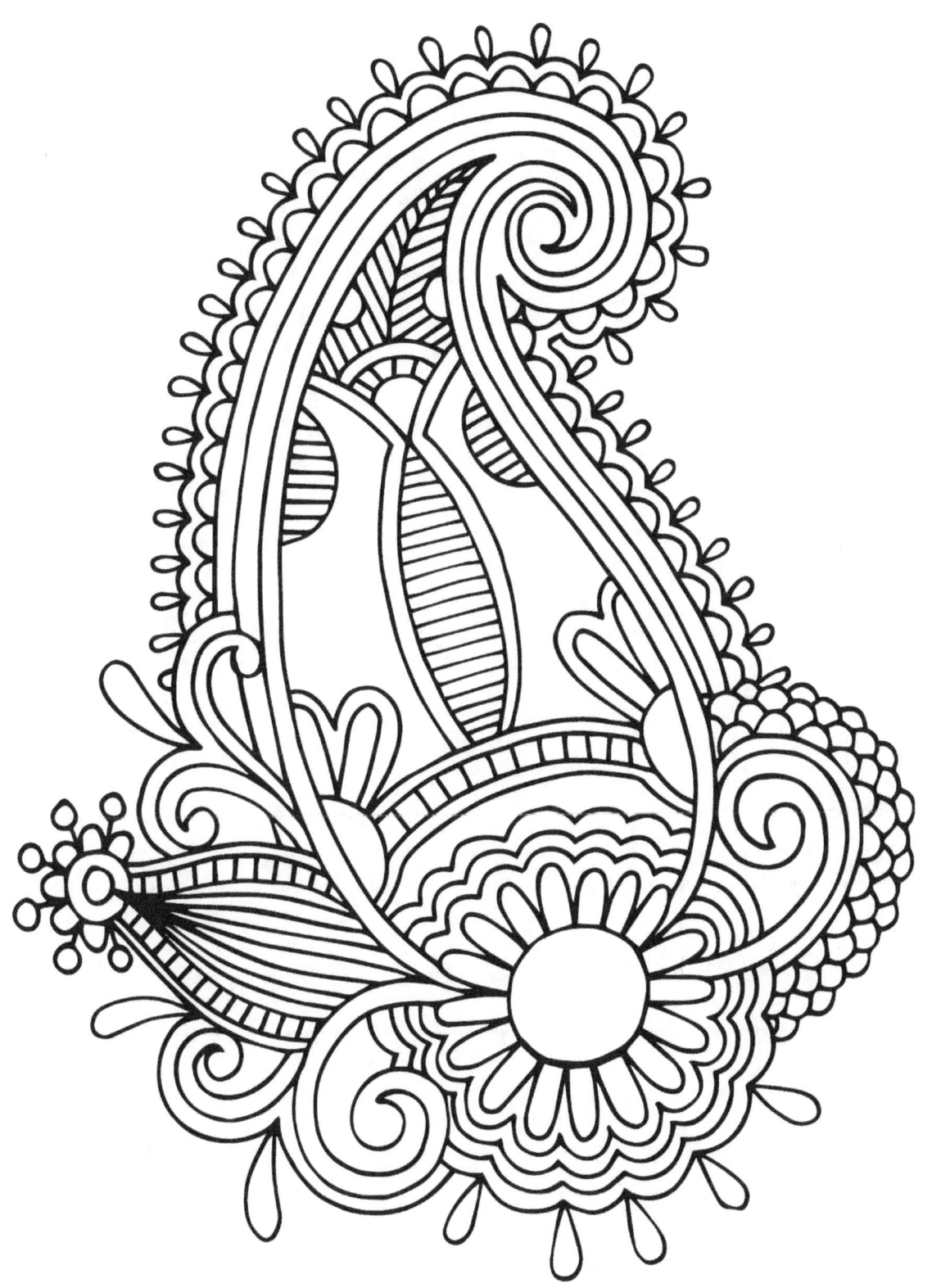

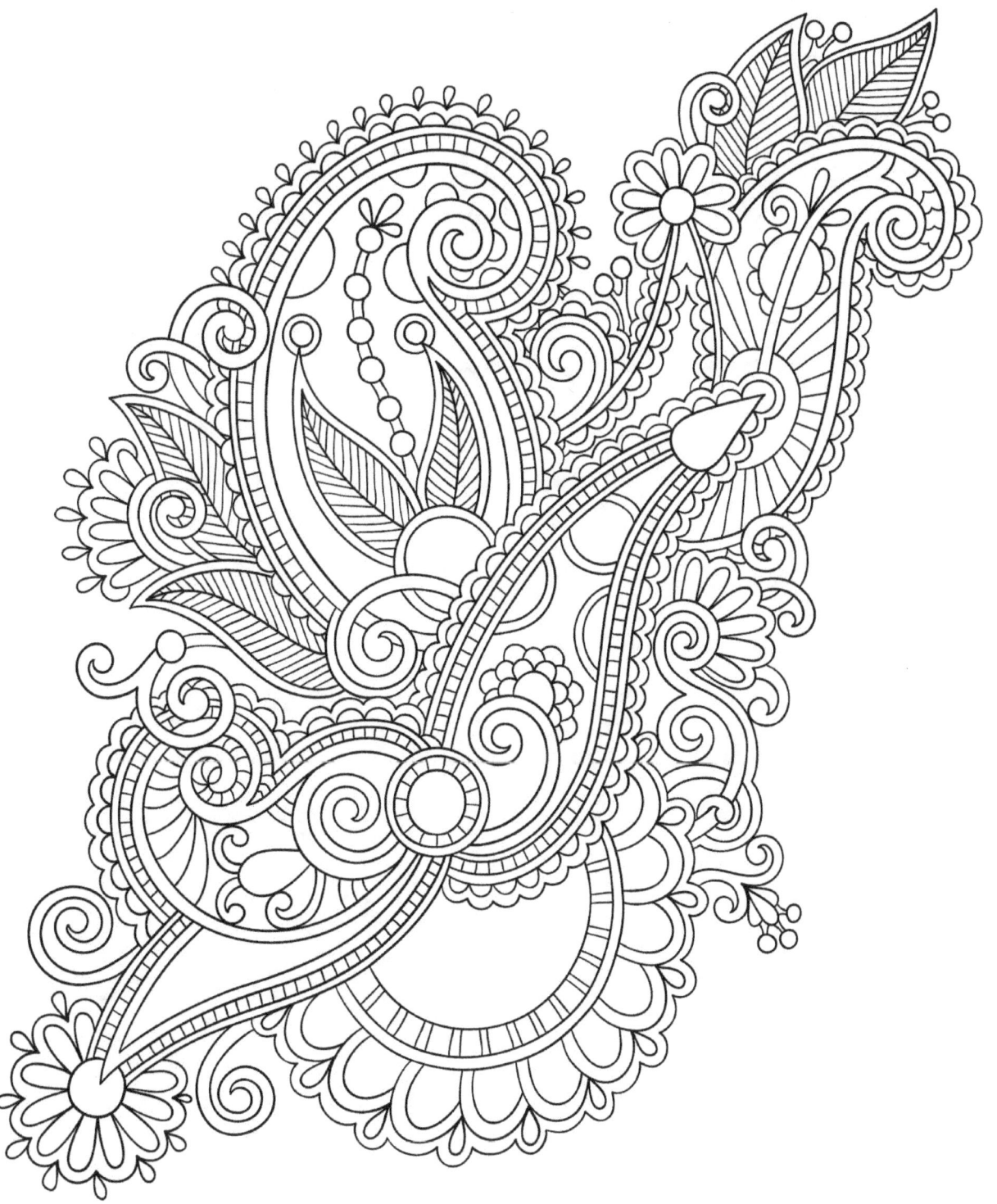

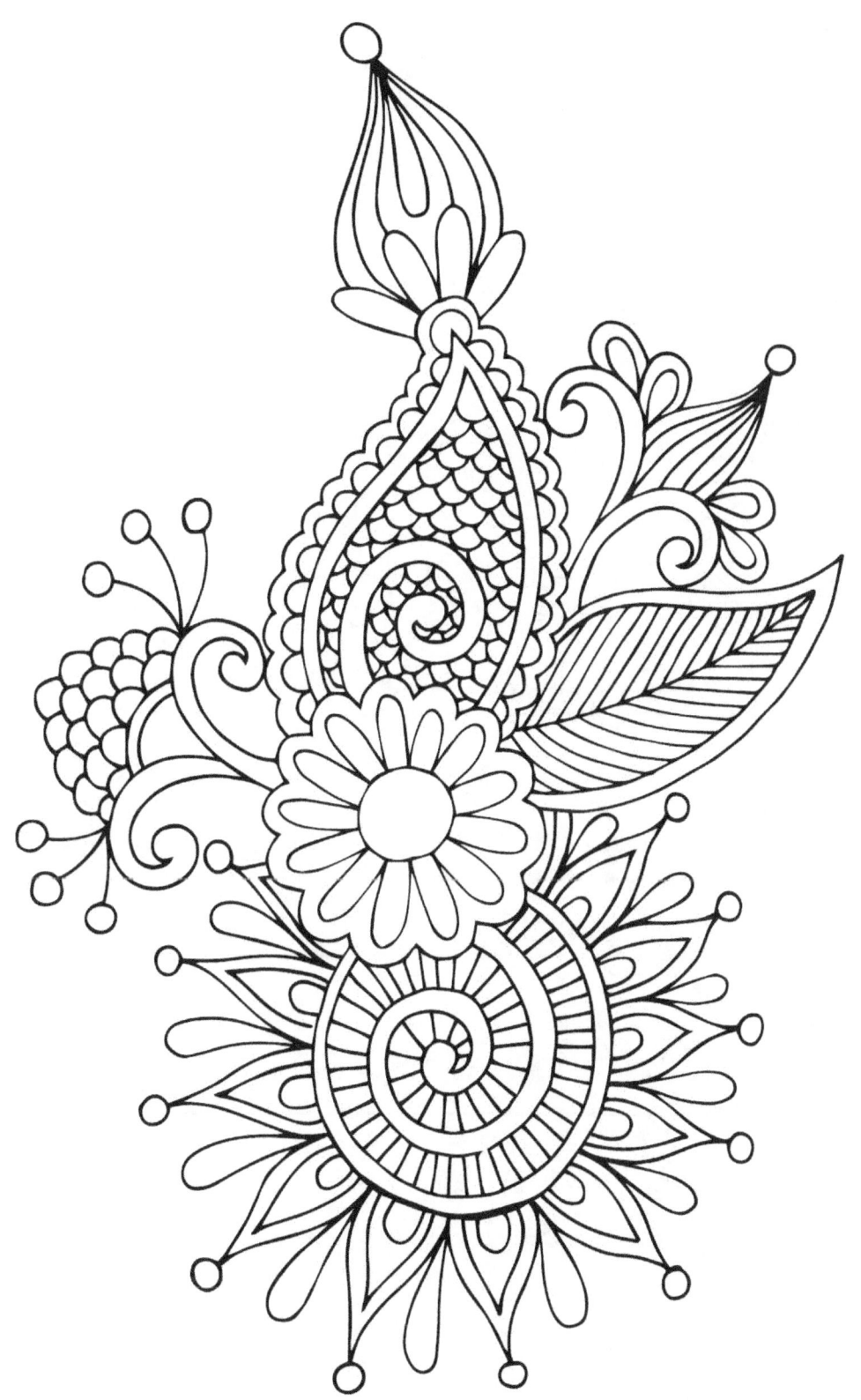

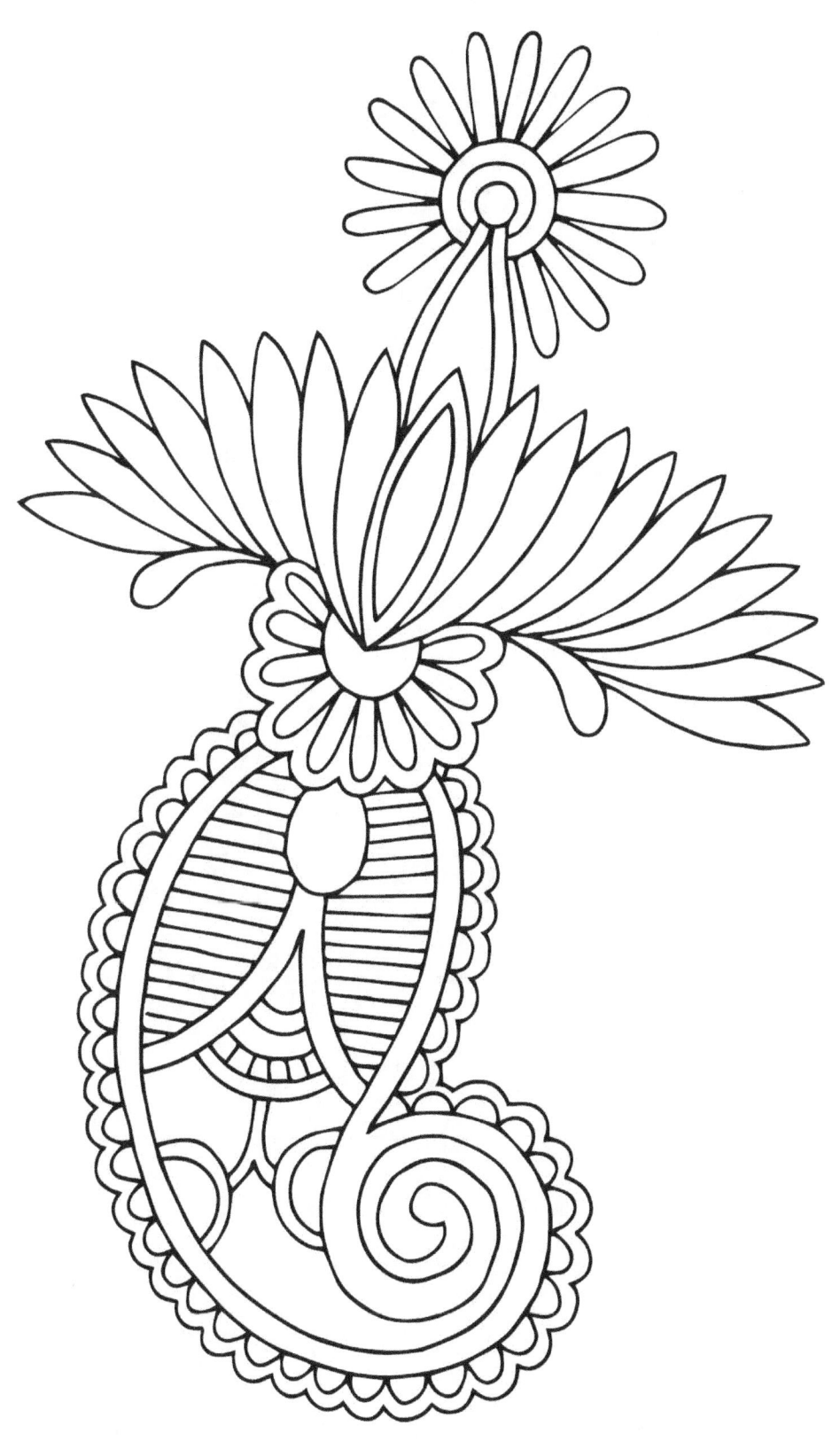

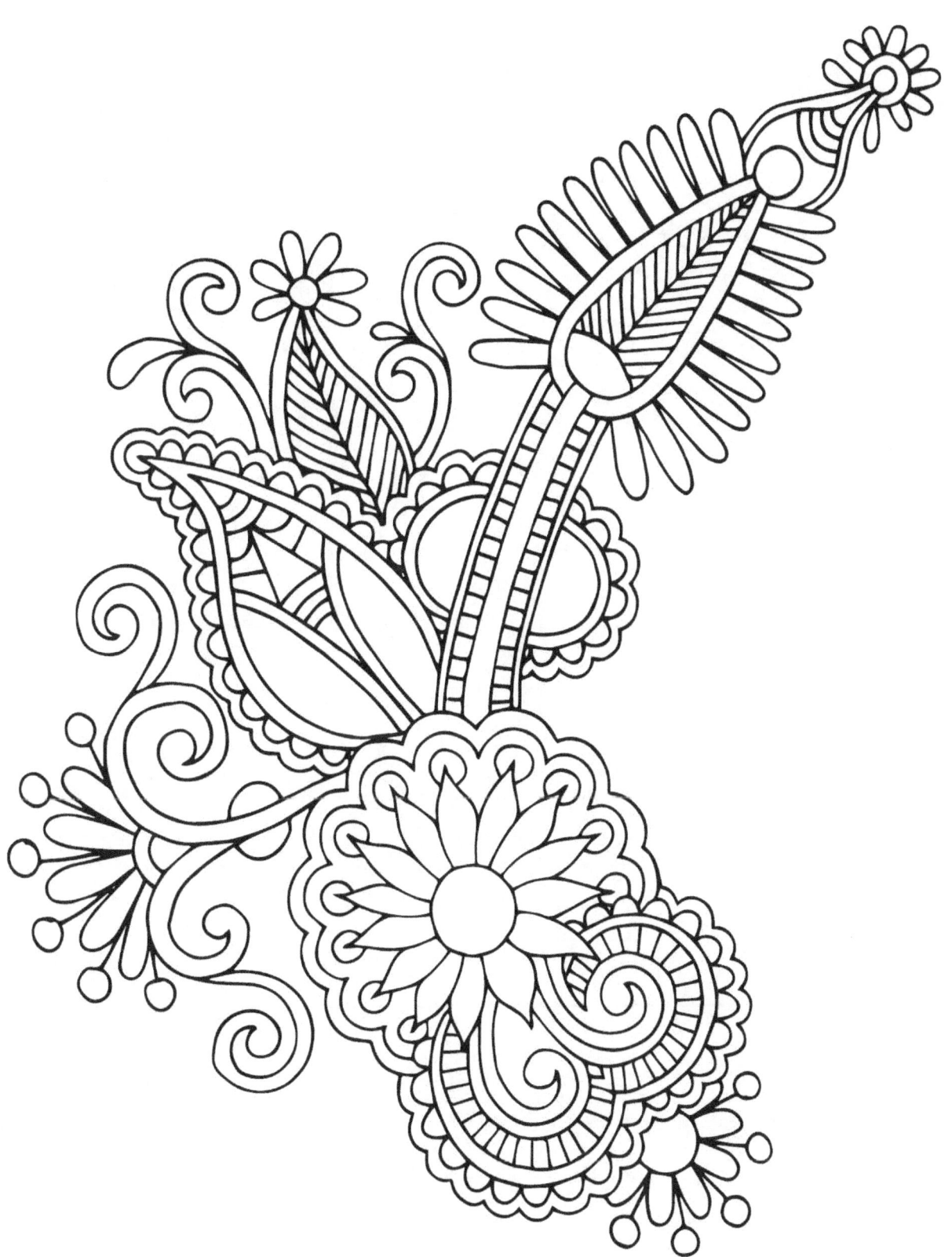

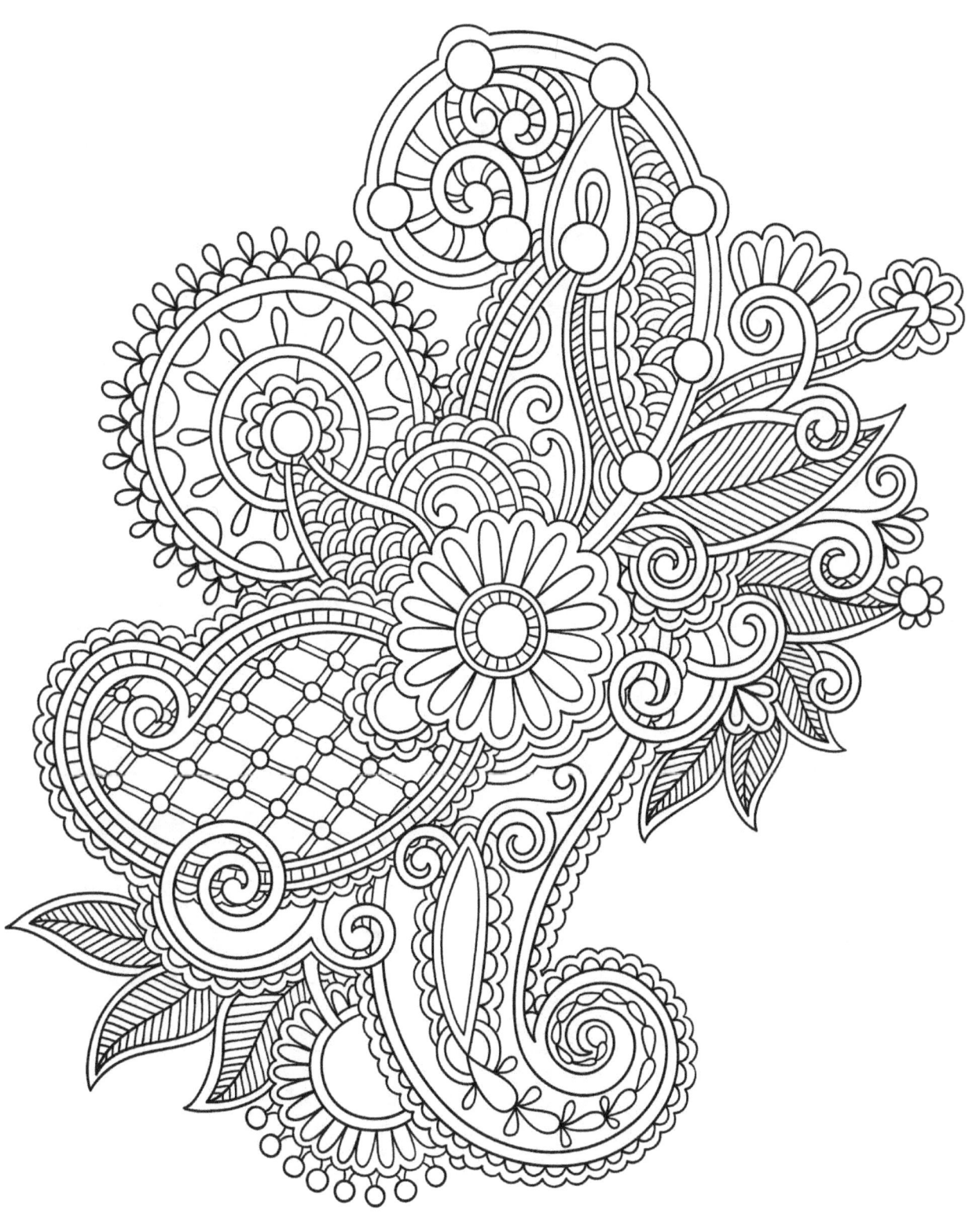

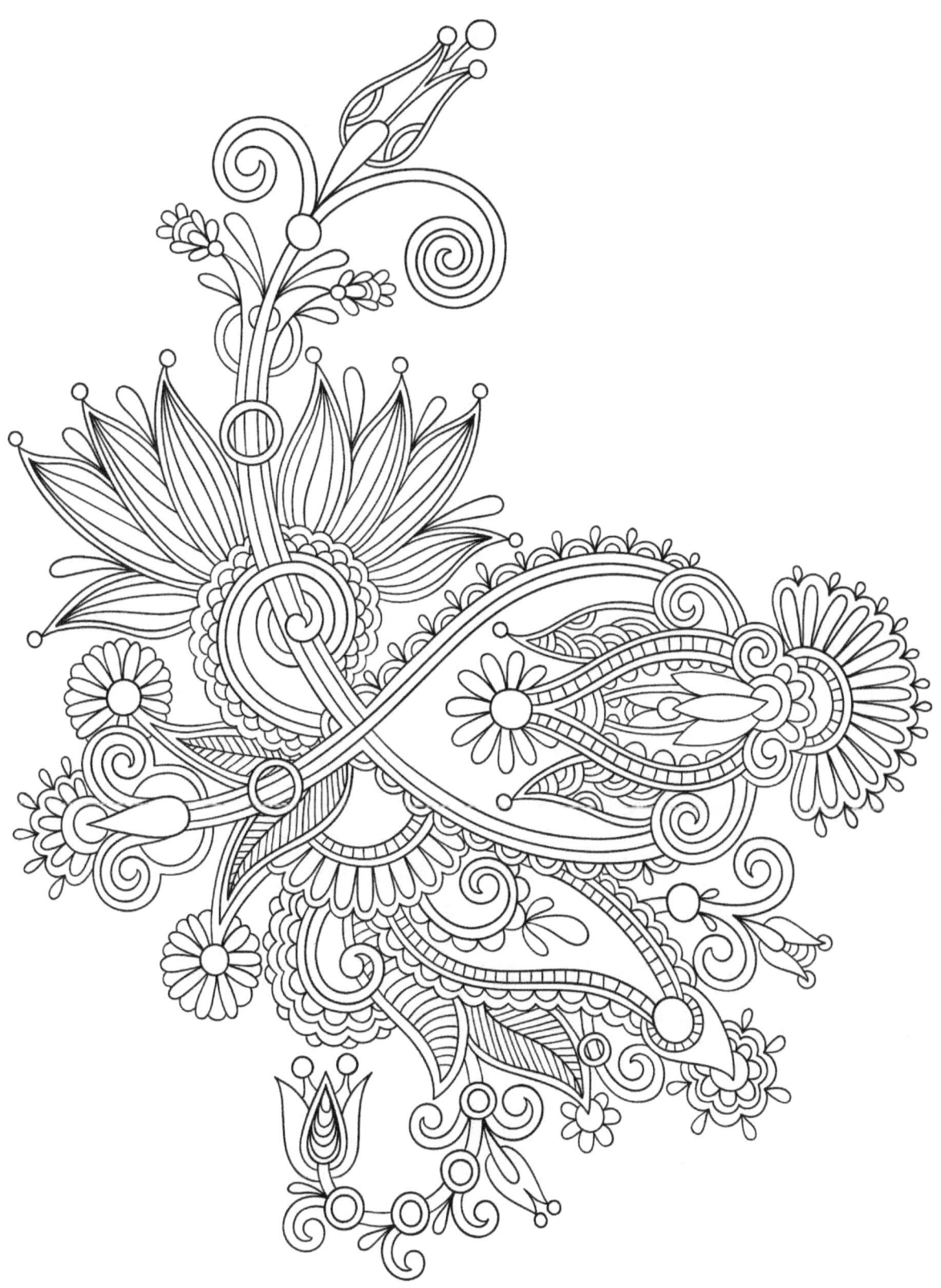

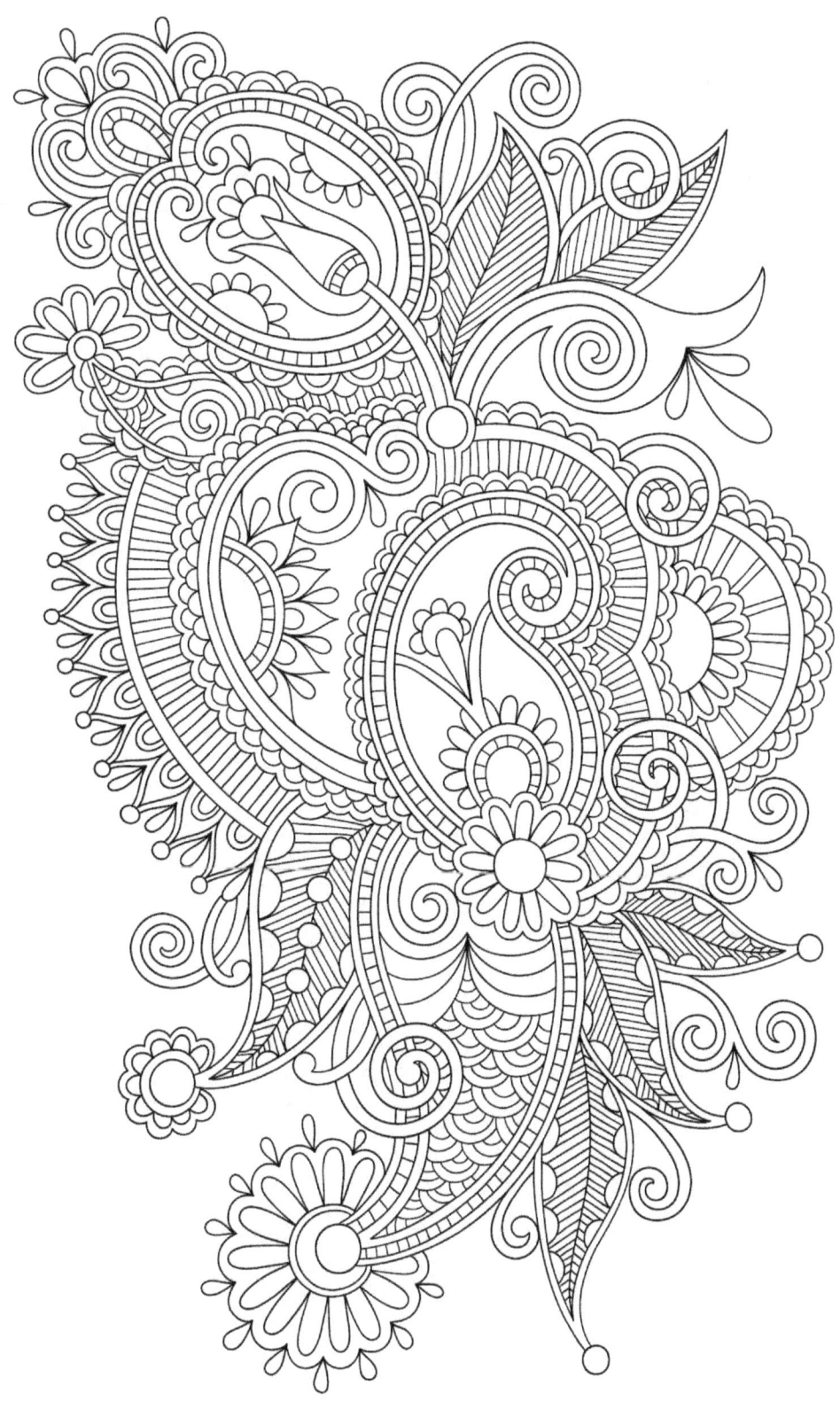

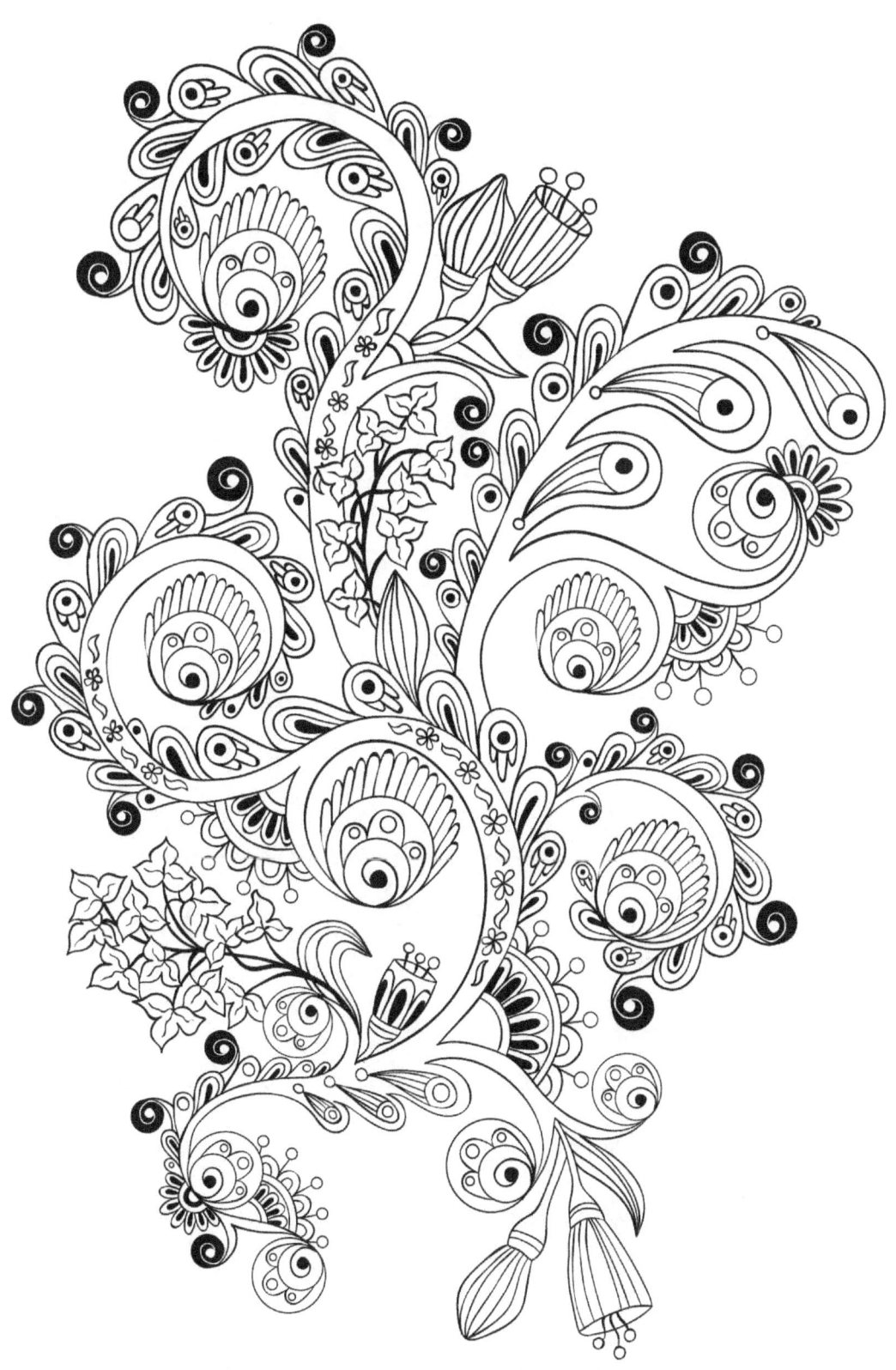

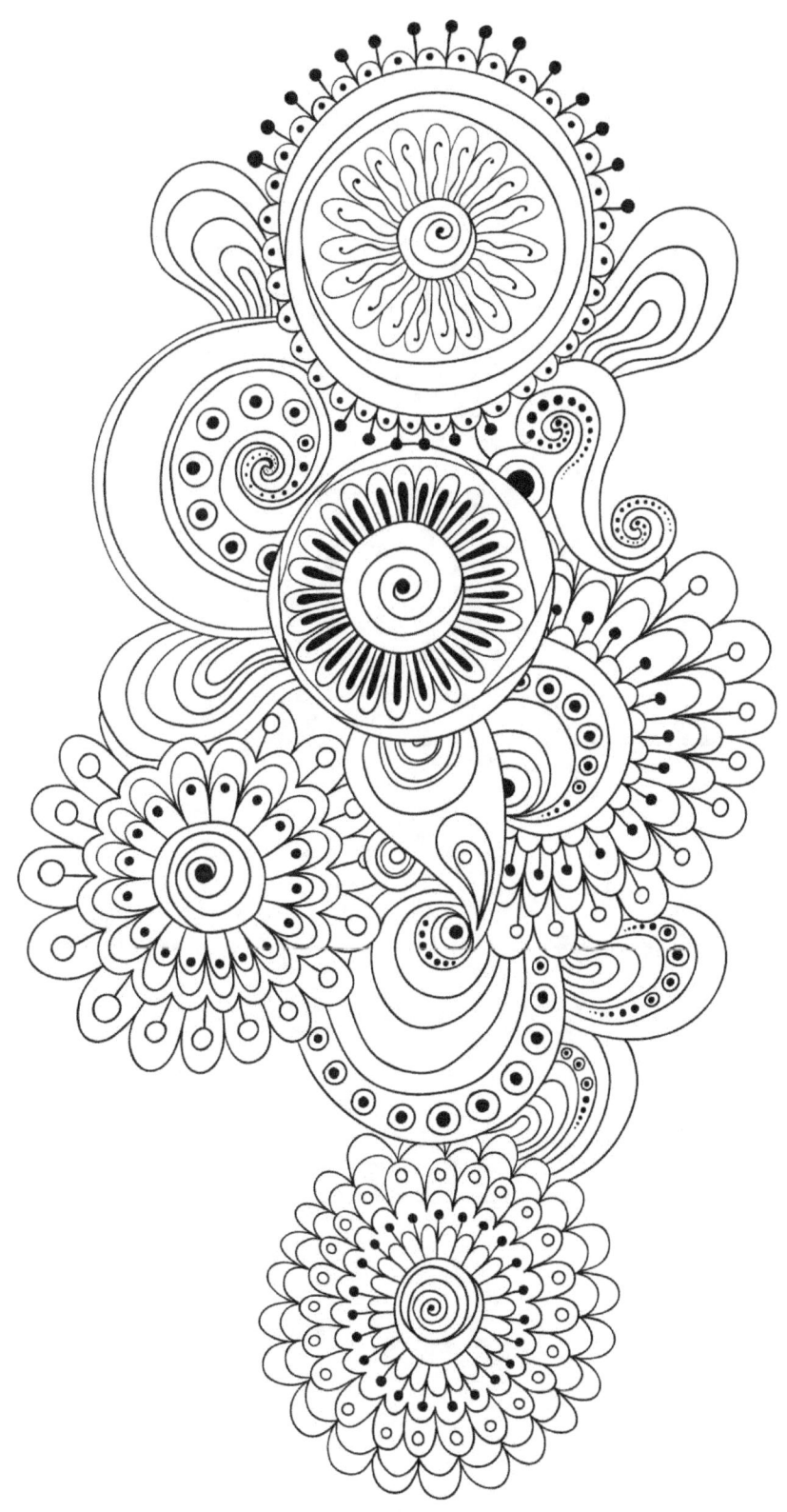

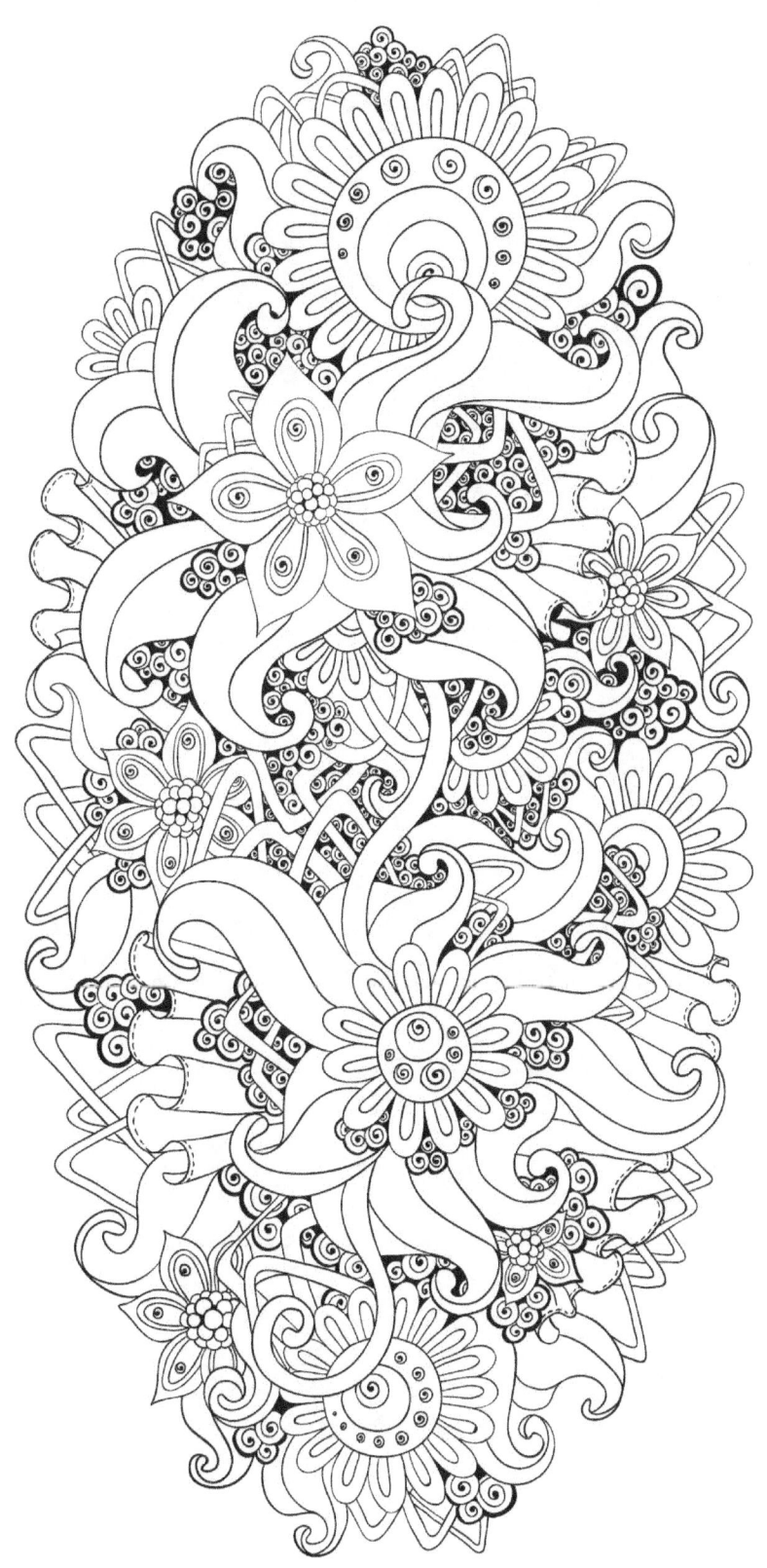

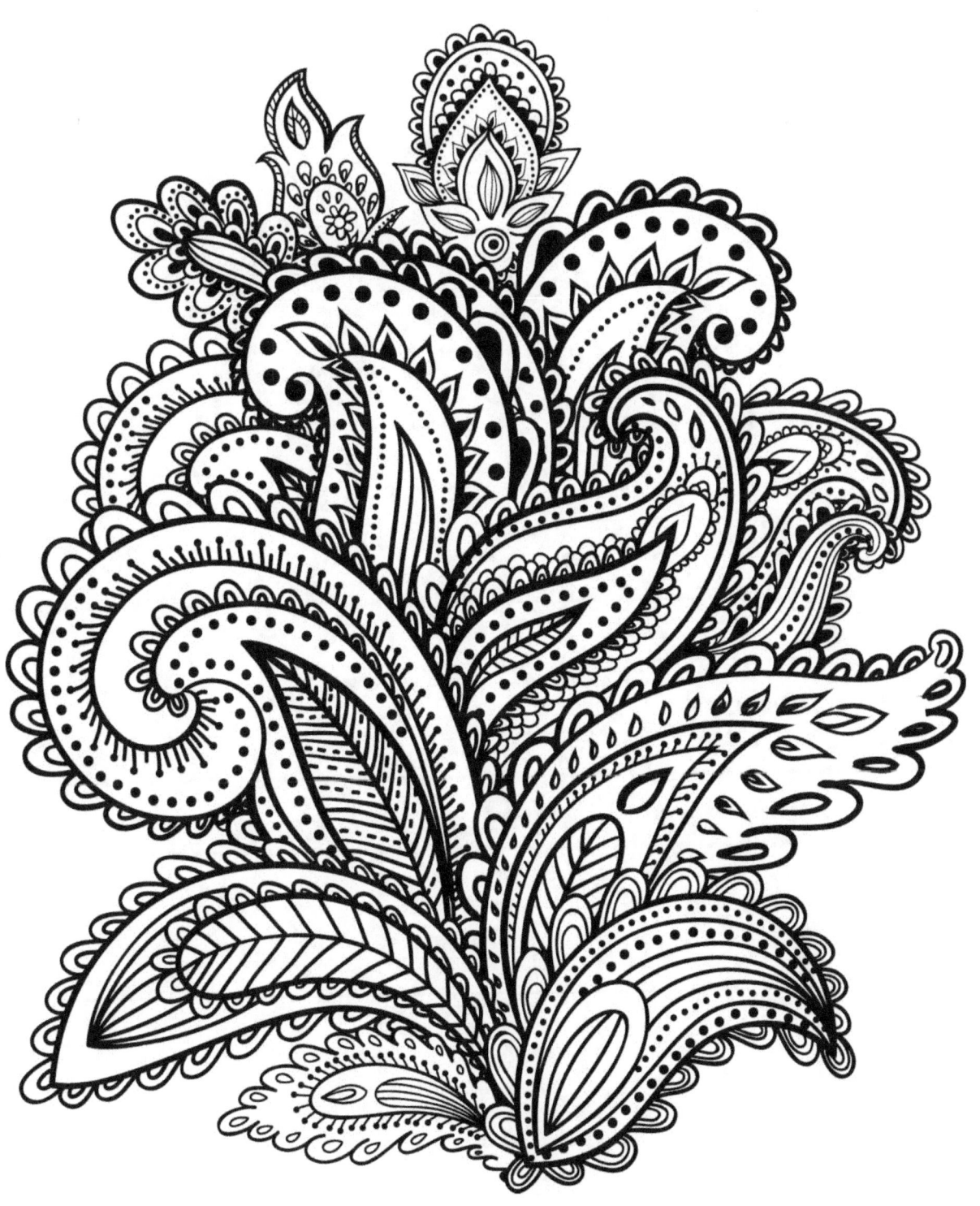

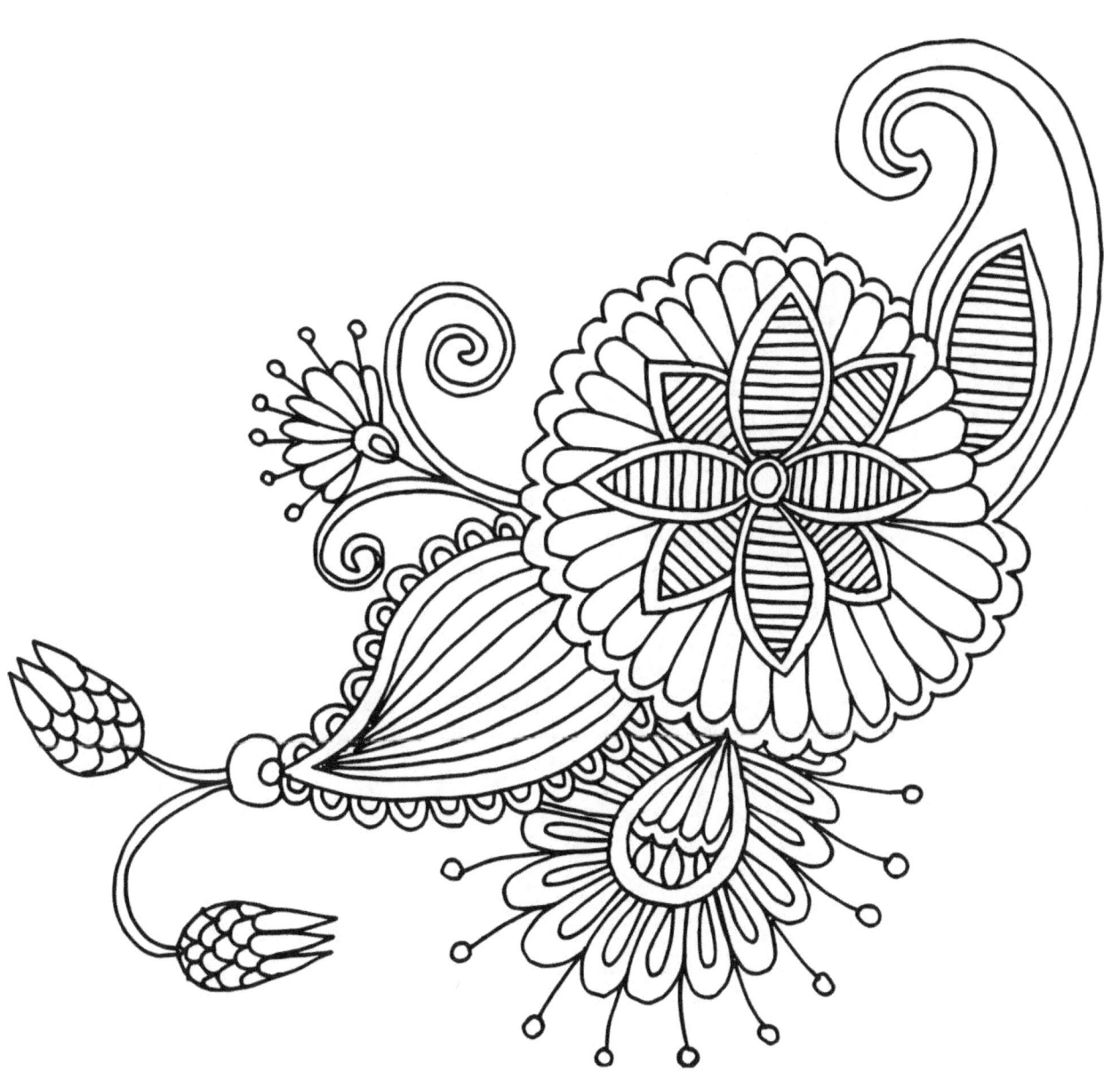

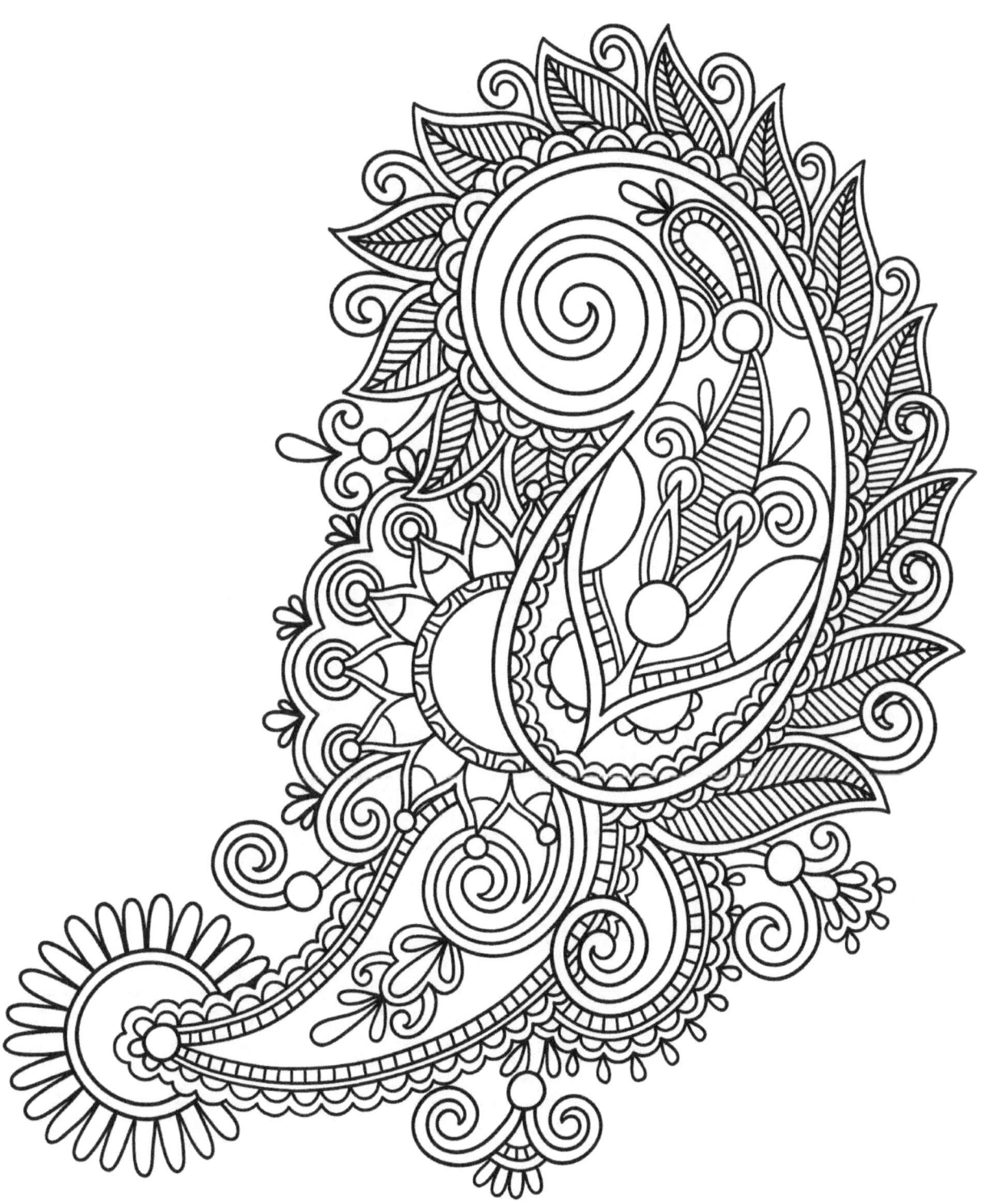

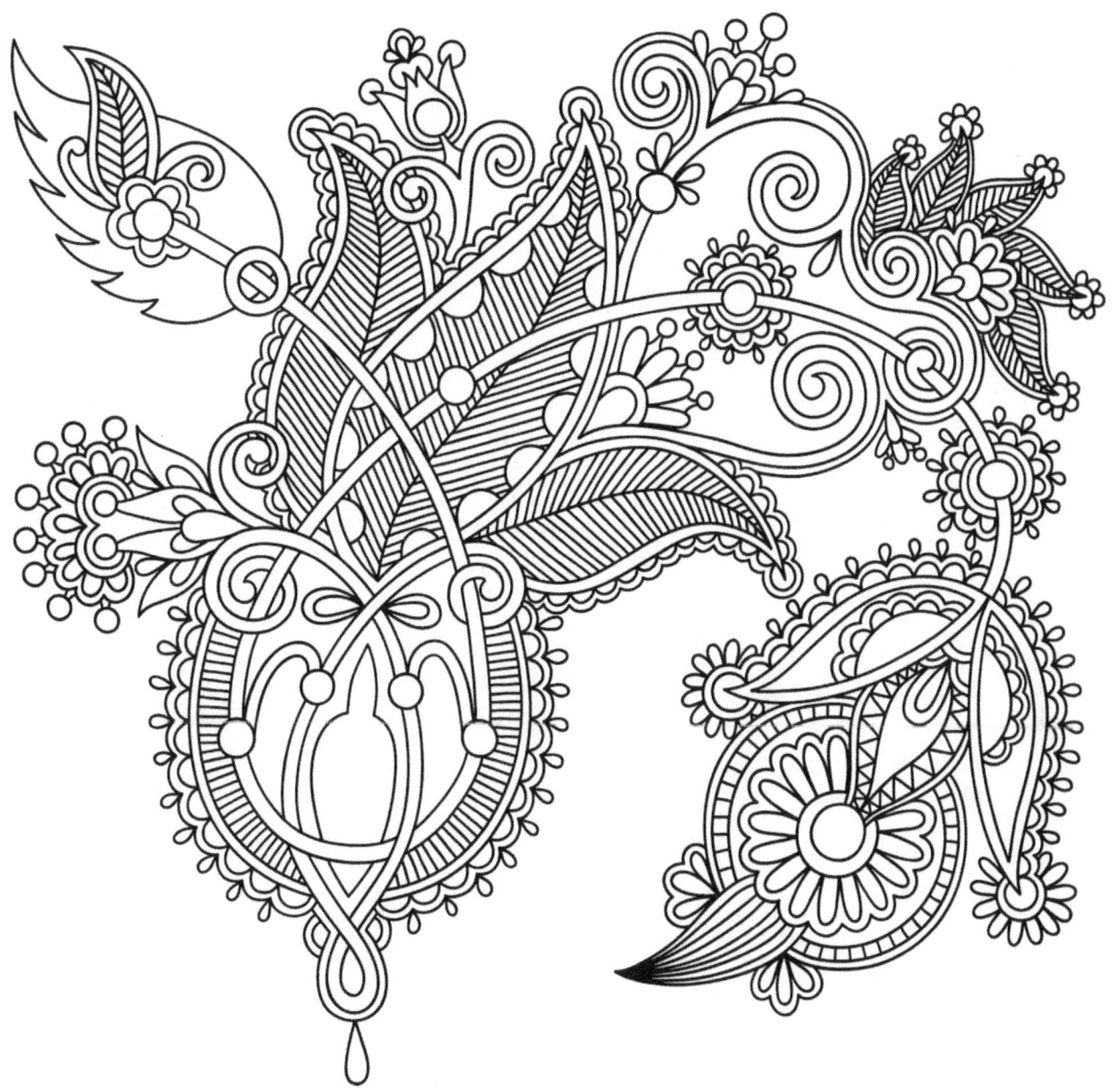

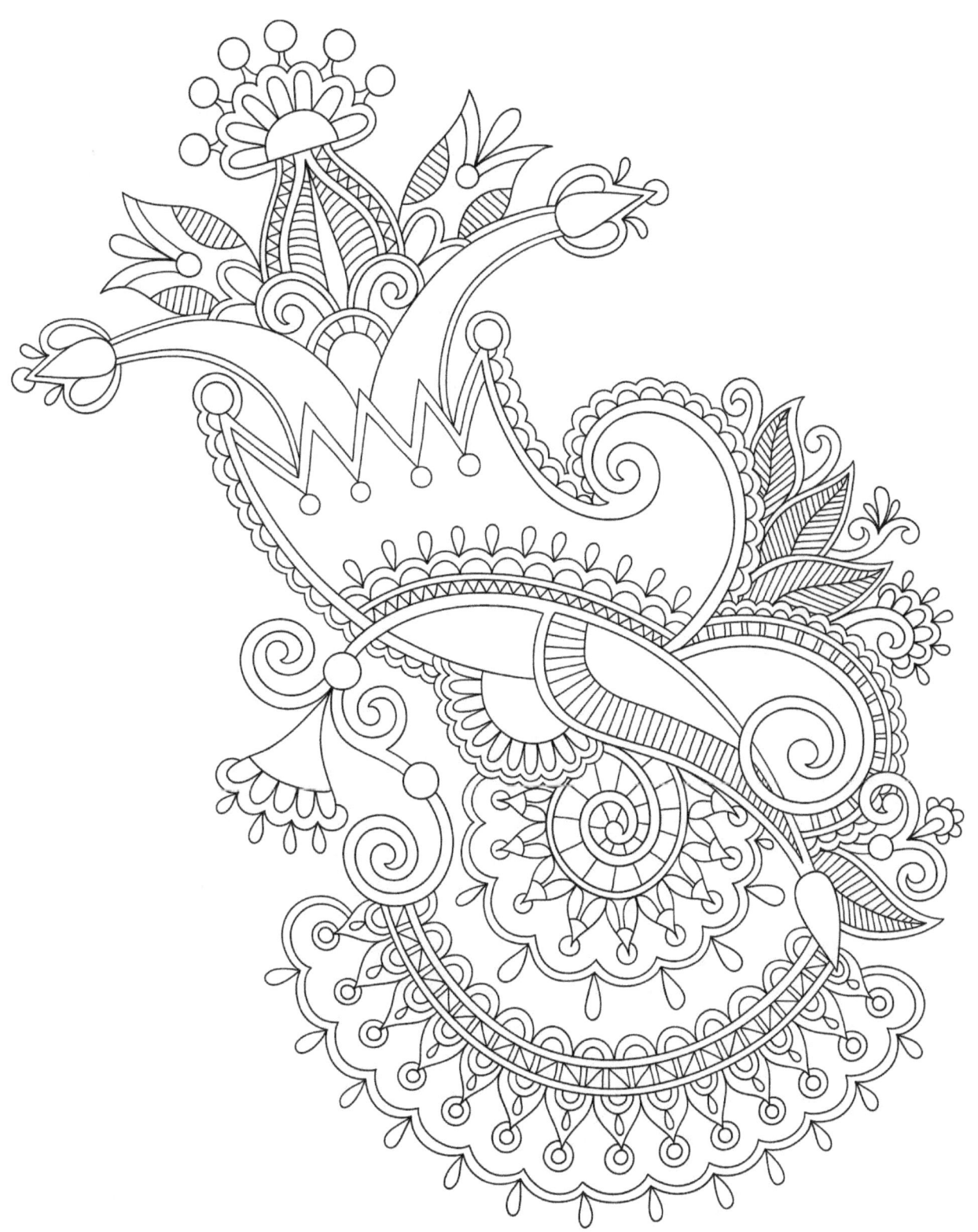

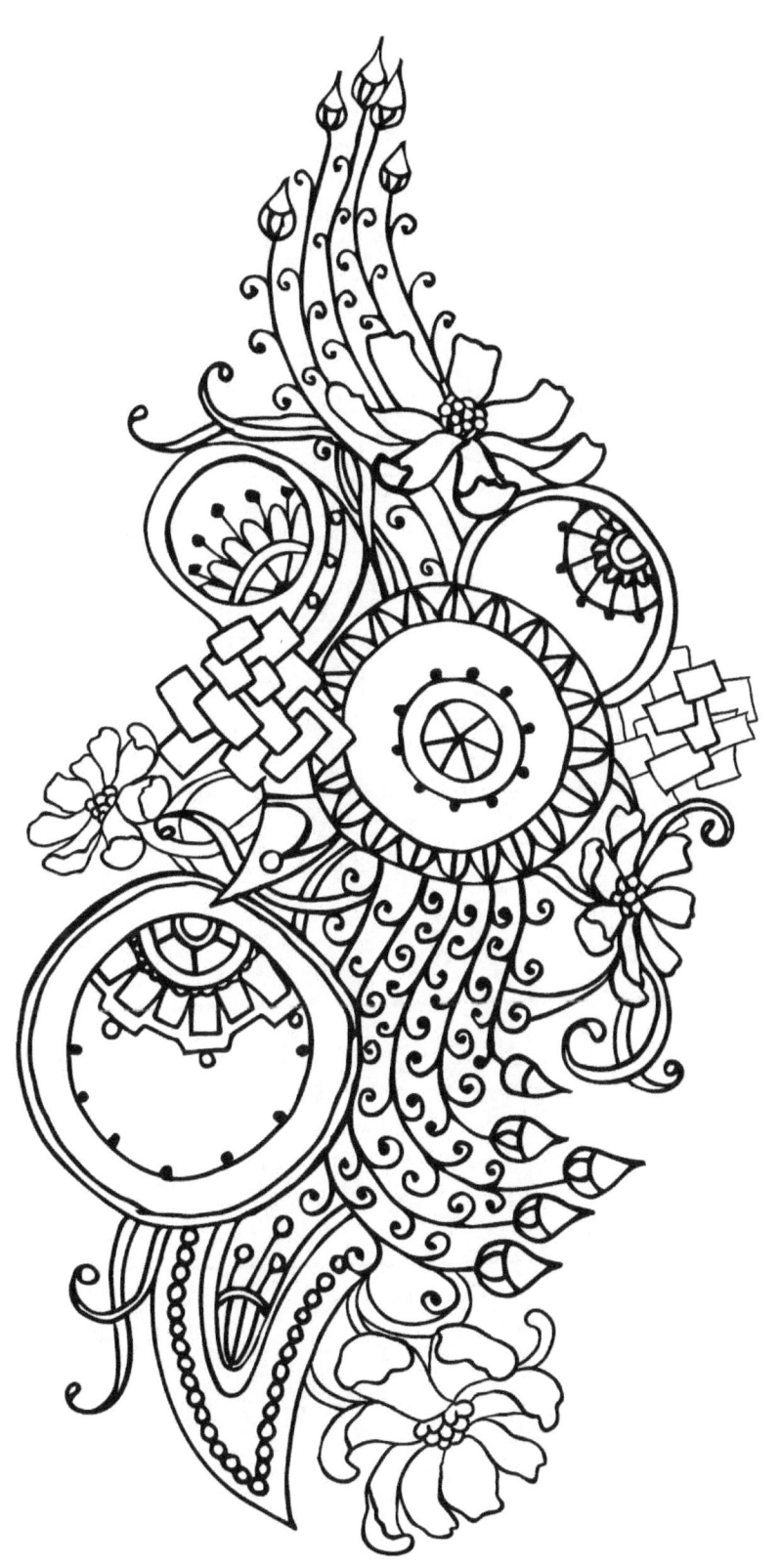

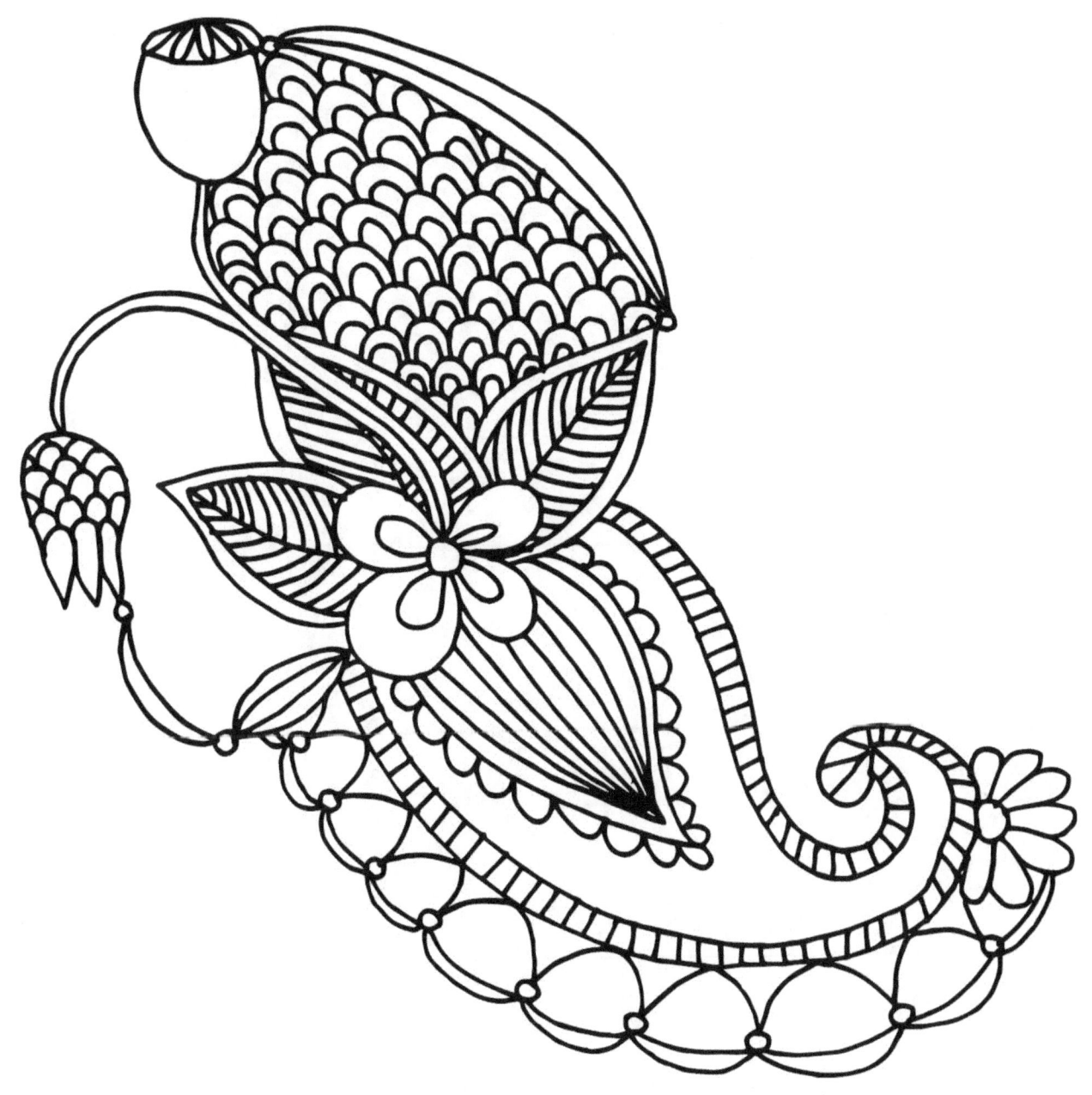

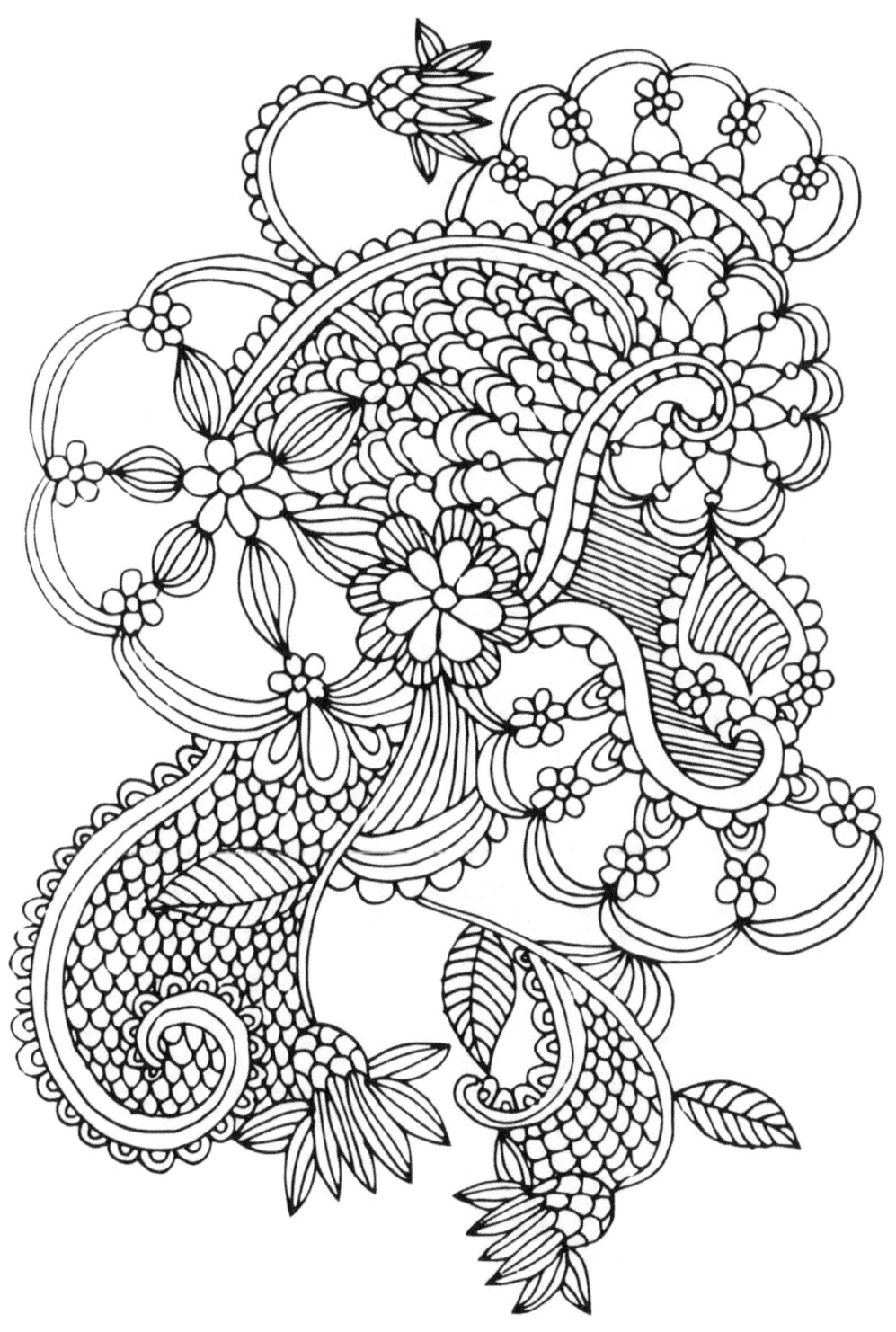

# More books from Hobby Habitat

You can find our entire Coloring Books collection on Amazon, just type in

**"Hobby Habitat Coloring Books"**

in the search box…or *search* for the books bellow by ISBN number!

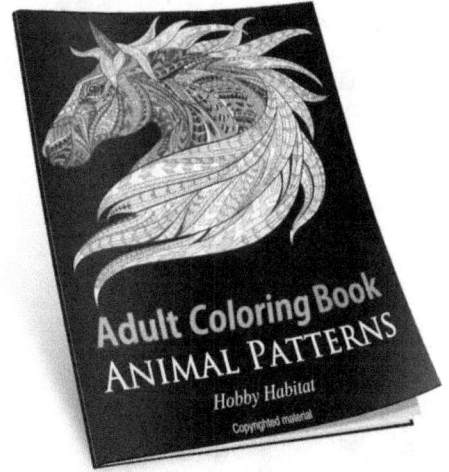

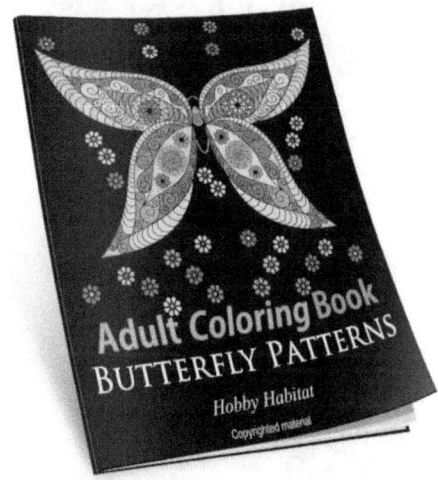

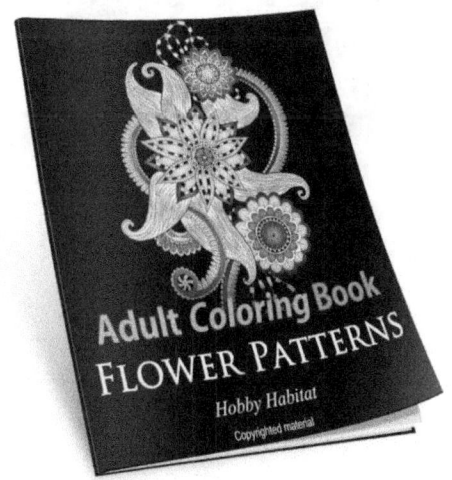

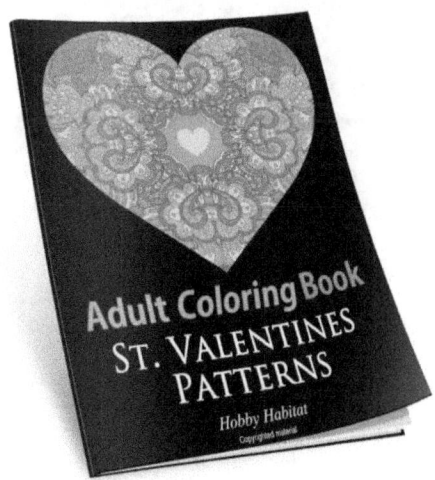

ISBN: 1522839542          ISBN: 1523607149

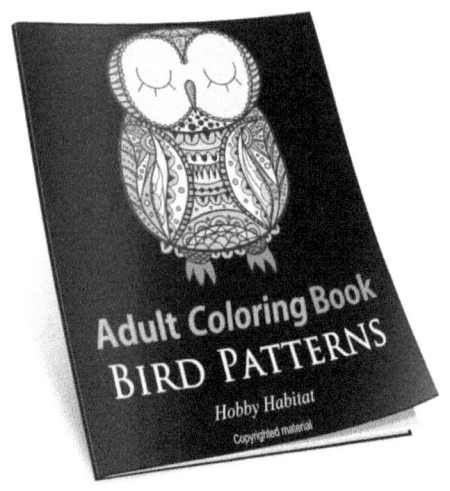

ISBN: 1523617411

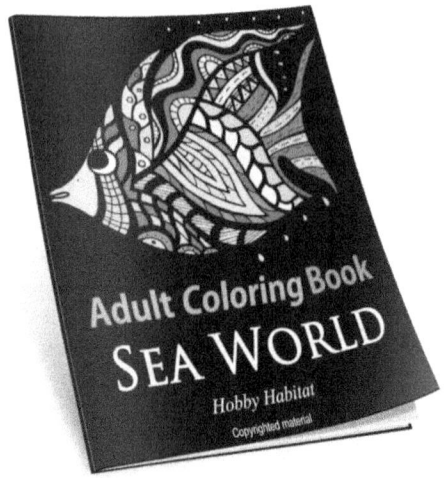

ISBN: 1523608544

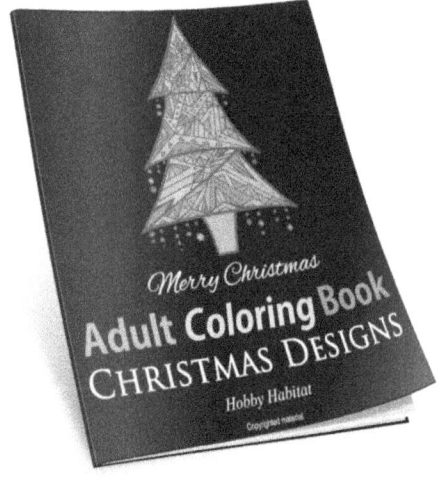
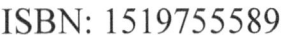

ISBN: 1519755589

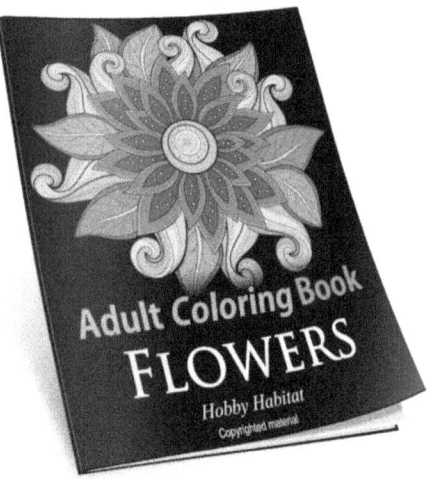

ISBN: 1523898917

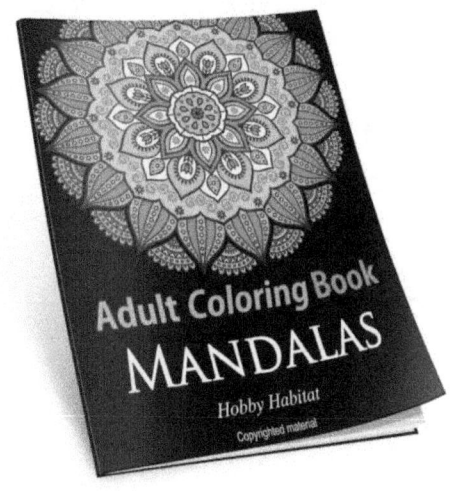

ISBN: 152389900X

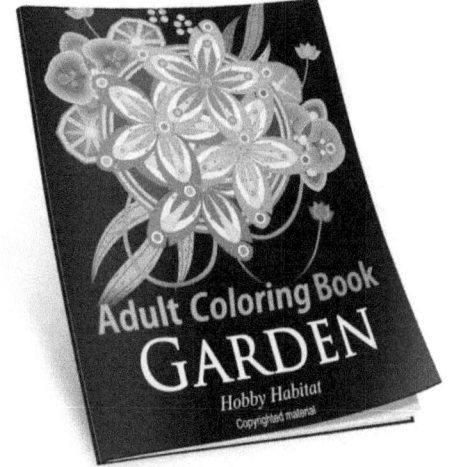

ISBN: 1530035554

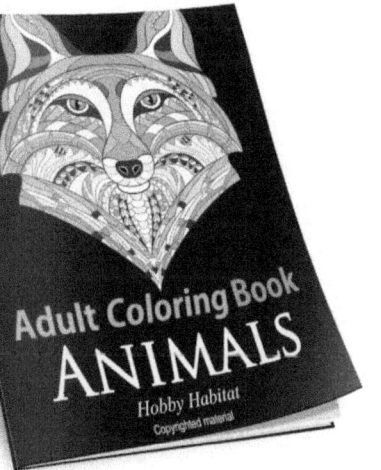

ISBN: 1530035473

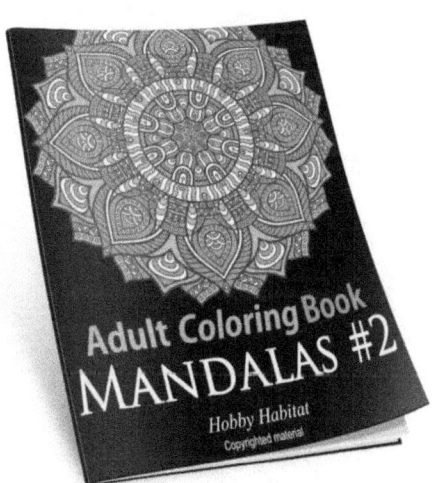

ISBN: 1530660955

# From the Author

Thank you for buying and coloring our book, we sincerely hope you have enjoyed it!

Can we ask for a small favor? A lot of work goes in to preparing and publishing our books and honest reviews really do help us, especially when it comes to understanding what we should improve in our books.

If you have a minute, we would really appreciate if you could go to the book store where you have purchased this book and leave a short review…we do actually read our reviews!

Thank you!

Remember also to grab your FREE bonus book at:

## www.hobbyhabitat.com/freecoloringbook